ML
385
.J66
1998

[SHERMA]

Touched by God : black gospel great

Meet the men and women who deliver God's
message in their powerful music, and
discover how they have been

TOUCHED BY GOD

"These near misses—these almost deaths—that's not
luck or some type of fantasy. That's the Lord telling you
that He has something in store for you. And I think it's
good to recognize that before you get hit by the truck, if
you know what I mean."

—John P. Kee

"It was the Lord speaking to me—I was certain of that.
He said, 'Slow down, Yolanda. Be still. Know that I am
still the same God that took care of you yesterday, and
all the years before. I did tell you that this is what you're
supposed to do, and because I told you, that should give
you enough reason to trust me.'"

—Yolanda Adams

"I just know that the talent He's given me is a pure thing
and it's not counterfeit or anything. It's from my heart."

—Donald Lawrence

"You know, to be perfectly honest with you, God works
on so many situations in my life, that I don't have too
much to ask anymore. He already knows. He just knows
my situations. He's just such an on-time God."

—Vickie Winans

For orders other than by individual consumers, Pocket Books grants a discount on the purchase of **10 or more** copies of single titles for special markets or premium use. For further details, please write to the Vice President of Special Markets, Pocket Books, 1230 Avenue of the Americas, 9th Floor, New York, NY 10020-1586.

For information on how individual consumers can place orders, please write to Mail Order Department, Simon & Schuster Inc., 100 Front Street, Riverside, NJ 08075.

TOUCHED BY GOD

Black Gospel Greats Share
Their Stories of Finding God

DR. BOBBY JONES
with LESLEY SUSSMAN

POCKET BOOKS
New York   London   Toronto   Sydney   Singapore

The sale of this book without its cover is unauthorized. If you purchased
this book without a cover, you should be aware that it was reported to
the publisher as "unsold and destroyed."   Neither the author nor the
publisher has received payment for the sale of this "stripped book."

 POCKET BOOKS, a division of Simon & Schuster Inc.
1230 Avenue of the Americas, New York, NY 10020

Copyright © 1998 by Dr. Bobby Jones and Lesley Sussman

Originally published in hardcover in 1998 by Pocket Books

All rights reserved, including the right to reproduce
this book or portions thereof in any form whatsoever.
For information address Pocket Books, 1230 Avenue
of the Americas, New York, NY 10020

ISBN: 0-671-02003-X

First Pocket Books trade paperback printing December 1999

10   9   8   7   6   5   4   3   2   1

POCKET and colophon are registered trademarks of
Simon & Schuster Inc.

Cover design by Matt Galemmo; front cover photo credits: Hezekiah
Walker courtesy of Verity Records; Albertina Walker courtesy of Verity
Records; Shirley Caesar © Evan Agostini; Miami Mass Choir © Savoy
Records/Andy Shefield

Printed in the U.S.A.

BP/✖

The love of my life has always been my mom. Her support and understanding of my desire to be a musical minister really encouraged and helped me to do what I do. Her constant counsel and love put me in a mental state of understanding my direction and why she brought me into this world, why the Lord sent me through her. I give it all back to her.

DISCARD

ACKNOWLEDGMENTS

I want to thank everyone in this God-driven industry who helped make this book possible—especially the gospel stars who so graciously contributed their valuable time.

Thanks to my dear friend and attorney, Richard Manson, who supported this project from its inception. Much gratitude, also, to Beverly Powell at Millennium Entertainment, who did the grunt work in making many of the initial contacts for this book, and Stephanie Williams, whose efforts are appreciated.

Special thanks to Jane Cavolina, my visionary editor at Pocket Books, for making this book happen, and my powerful literary agent, Claire Gerus. Claire, I love you!

Touched by God would be nothing more than a great idea if it weren't for the enormous contribution of Les Sussman, the only Jewish guy I know who once tried to convince his rabbi to have his temple organist play some gospel tunes. The many hours Les spent helping me to conduct the interviews and getting this book in shape were of invaluable assistance.

Thanks, also, to Eugene Corey of Brave New Words, for his excellent transcription skills, as well as the helpful staff at the Harlem Center for Reading and Writing.

On a very personal note, I want to thank my recently deceased mother, Mrs. Augusta Jones, my sister, Lula

Puckett, and my brother, James Jones, for their love, support, and just being there.

Other dear friends I wish to acknowledge are: Ethel, Sonnetta, Vickie, Debbie, Tommy, Shirley, Meridith, Dettick, Terry, Simeon, Aretha Franklin, Maya Angelou, Jesse Jackson, Barbara Mandrell, Wayne Newton, LaMar, Terrell, Alonzo, Peggy, Shirley W., Vanessa Bell, Merdean, Carol, Al, Pastor Bonnie, and countless others.

If I didn't list your name, it only meant that I couldn't remember everyone—I'm getting older, remember?

And we, clay, *touched by God,*
will reach out for holiness,
and exclaim in wonder. . . .
—ANCIENT HEBREW SCRIPTURE

CONTENTS

PREFACE

The Lord will use any soldier that wants to be used in His glorious army.

I like to identify gospel singers as brave soldiers—or warriors—on the battlefield. That identification suggests that gospel artists have the world as their battlefield and are part of an army that cannot have too many soldiers.

In *Touched by God* I share with you a series of inspiring conversations with some of my personal friends in the gospel music industry who have pushed forward to become outstanding, identifiable artists and masters of their craft.

Over the years, as host of my *Bobby Jones Gospel* and *Video Gospel* television shows, which air on the Black Entertainment Network, the Odyssey Television Network, and on television stations in other nations throughout the world such as England, Nigeria, Japan, and Uganda, I have had the rare pleasure of meeting all the artists who appear in this book.

All of them have been touched by God in their own lives, as you will be when you read and share these heartfelt, God-inspired stories. They all have been selected because they are witness to the anointing and guidance of the Holy Spirit.

When the troops are brought together to present their messages to the people willing to hear the Word, it is important that each soldier understand his or her role and go forth to battle with the anointing and guidance of the Holy Spirit.

The performers in this book all have done so.

There are several forms or styles of gospel music used to save, inspire, motivate, heal, and encourage the believers and the nonbelievers of the coming of Jesus Christ and our way to the promised land.

The singers and songwriters I have selected for inclusion in this book are artists representing styles from the traditional to the urban contemporary gospel sound. I highly respect each of them and chose them because, in my opinion, they have very much influenced the gospel music industry.

In hearing their testimonies, I was thrilled to no end that readers of this book would also come to realize the power and the work that the Lord has for each of us as we go forth.

When, for example, I first talked to Reverend James Moore about his poor physical condition and how he keeps on traveling and spreading the Word despite his blindness and related health problems, it was evident from his response that he was touched by God.

I know that you will certainly want to read his moving account of how doctors gave him only a few months to live, but the Lord had a different prognosis in mind for the faith-driven performer.

The "Queen of Gospel," Albertina Walker, has walked by my side for many years now as, together, we continue to develop a path for more of God's soldiers to follow.

Albertina's descriptive language leaves one spellbound as this legendary artist describes the many trials and tribulations she has faced over the years, and how God has helped her overcome such adversity.

Daryl Coley shared with me his moving story of two occasions when God delivered him—once when he wanted to break free of a lifestyle of alcohol and drugs and, a second time, when he became severely depressed over the brutal murder of his best friend and mentor.

Vickie Winans, LaShun Pace, Dottie Peoples, Vanessa Bell Armstrong, Shirley Caesar, and Dorothy Norwood are all outstanding female gospel messengers. All will bring you moments of sheer joy when they share their experiences of how their faith was challenged before being touched by God.

Kirk Franklin was first brought to my attention by his new Gospo Centric record label executive at the time, Vickie Mack Lataillade. We did a television taping of *Bobby Jones Gospel* in the summer of 1994 in Atlanta, Georgia, and there was no space for Kirk at that particular taping.

So Vickie asked me to please consider making a space available, which I did. And Kirk was allowed to deliver his message. The participants in the show and the fans were really blown away with his presentation of "The Reason Why We Sing," followed by "He Able."

Those moments were another step in the beginning of a great soldier's exposure to the world. In his dramatic testimony, Kirk talks about how the Lord saved him from his violent lifestyle in Fort Worth's black ghetto, so that he could go on to spread the Gospel through his amazing musical ministry.

Hezekiah Walker, John P. Kee, Donald Lawrence, Mark Kibble, Reverend Milton Biggham, Doug Williams, and Kurt Carr are all relatively young soldiers for Christ, with powerful testimonies and messages of hope and salvation to share with you.

I know that when you read these and the other inspiring true accounts in this book, that you, too, will be blessed and encouraged to have faith and trust in the Lord. Like these great masters of music, we can all of us be touched by God if we open our hearts to Him. . . .

Dr. Bobby Jones
Nashville, Tennessee
May 1998

Touched by God

REV. JAMES MOORE

Photo by LaBass Photography, Jackson, MS

I consider James one of my best friends. The uniqueness of James doesn't stop with his vocalization, which is very strong, and very steady, and very experienced.

He's been in the Church of God movement all of his life and certainly knows how to sing Christian music. He loves to share his background and tell about how he was influenced by the late Dr. Mattie Moss Clark and others from the city of Detroit, where he got his first push in gospel music.

But what continues to make James so unique is that even with his physical disabilities, he continues to push and go forward and do unusual things that even people in good health won't do.

And I think that's what makes him so special. It's not just his wonderful vocalization, but his desire to want to continue to do what he's always done—even while he grapples with his current illness.

As far as performance goes, James is one of the best. He may not have his eyesight, but he sees the Lord as well as any soldier in the gospel army.

May he continue to be touched by God!

*A*lthough the Rev. James Moore is afflicted with diabetic blindness and life-threatening kidney disease, neither has stopped the widely acclaimed gospel star and ordained minister from proclaiming himself the victor rather than the victim.

"It ain't over 'til God says it's over," exclaims the chart-topping Malaco Records artist. James goes even further, confidently predicting that one day soon the Lord will bless him with a complete healing.

That kind of unswerving faith in the Lord has always marked the life of this Detroit native, who, since beginning his recording career in 1993, has racked up an impressive variety of awards—including four Stellars, the highest award in gospel music.

Even when the soul-filled vocalist lost three of his younger siblings in a tragic house fire, and later, after his dearest friend and mentor died of cancer, James caught his spiritual balance by turning to heaven, viewing such misfortune as the Lord's way of testing his faith.

The gospel star's moving account of his battle against his debilitating eye and kidney disease is also a testimonial to real living faith.

"I just felt like God was allowing these things to happen to me to see how much I really loved Him," he declares with the patience of Job. "These were all tests—trials—and I wasn't about to throw my hands up and lose my faith. I love Him too much for that. I'm a victor, not a victim, in life and I'll trust in the Lord until I die."

Life first began pulling the rug from under James Moore's feet when he was just an infant. His mother, an unwed seventeen-year-old, was unable to raise her first of ten children, so at her aunt's urging, she turned James over to a foster family for his upbringing.

Even today, James refuses to bear a grudge against his mother. "Mama was just seventeen and she was in a very precarious situation," he says in her defense. "I know she didn't want to give me to one of the members of the church, but she was in a very tough situation."

James continues defending his mother by emphasizing that she was a morally upright person. "My mom had always been a church young lady—she was raised in the church.

"That's where my foster mother met her. She said to my mother, 'Shirley, I'll take James if you want me to take him.' So that's how that came about."

It was from his foster parents that James grew up learning to love and fear the Lord.

"They were religious people who had their own family, and they were steady churchgoers," he recalls. "So I was raised in the church. All I knew was the church. And there was lots of spiritual talk about God at home. My foster mother would always talk about the Lord, what God can do.

"She was the kind of woman that would get happy in a minute by talking about God. And my real mom would visit and I would get spiritual talk from my mom, too. So I had a good training ground for the church and for God, Himself, even though I didn't know God back then the way I know Him now."

Sharing memories of his childhood, the gifted singer remembers growing up on the east side of Detroit, the "hotbed" of gospel music. He doesn't recall the neighborhood as a particularly tough one.

"There were, you know, black and white families," he relates. "But after a while the whites started to move out because more blacks were moving in. Still, it stayed a good neighborhood because it was a family neighborhood. A majority of the homes were two-family flats."

James portrays himself as a well-behaved youngster, a quiet kind of kid who always took a keen interest in religion. "I wasn't a wild kid," he says with a smile. "I was a kid who was very curious about certain things. I was always very fond of the preaching of the gospel in church and also the singing and the music."

The youngster gave an early display of his own talent when, at age seven, he sang for the first time before his church congregation. That memory elicits a chuckle from James.

"I can still remember that they stood me up on a little box, and my first song was 'How Great Art Thee.' And all the people who heard it were elated. The folks really enjoyed it. I had the people dancin' and clappin'. But I don't think I gave any thought to going professional until I was about eighteen years old."

The years passed by rather uneventfully until high school, James recalls, a time when the teenager's relationship with his foster parents began to deteriorate.

"As I got older, living with my foster parents, we started having a few problems," he relates. "And those problems stemmed from the fact that they had their own daughter and grandchildren.

"And I looked at that and, being a teenager, I just felt like I needed to get a chance to know more about my side of the family. I just wanted to be with my mother and my sisters and my brothers. So I was kind of rebellious."

There was something else that contributed to the ill feelings between him and his foster family. Whenever the teenager would bring up the subject of his real mother, his foster parent would launch into a negative tirade about her, something James remembers he didn't want to hear.

"My foster mother was real sweet, but sometimes she would say negative things about my mom. And it got to a point that I got tired of it. And when I said something about that, I got a beating by her husband. He worked at the Ford Motor Company."

There was one particular night that James painfully recalls being "beat buck-naked with switches." He also remembers fleeing his house in terror. "I was running through the streets there on the East Side with no shoes on, just my underwear. And the police saw me, and they took me to the youth detention home."

Although the police did their best to urge the teenager to return home, James refused to do so. "I didn't want to go back because the relationship was no longer a relationship. All I was hearing back there was, 'You'll never be nothing.' 'Your Mama wasn't nothing.' My foster mother would always throw that up in my face."

For the next several months, James called a youth detention center his home. Although it wasn't the best of living situations, he recollects that it was still better than the abuse he'd been receiving at home.

James also recalls finding solace and inspiration in the gospel music he would listen to when he felt down or lonely. "All my life I've loved that kind of music," he submits. "I'd been listening to it and singing gospel music since I was seven years old, when I gave my first solo in church."

One day, while walking around the city, James discovered Detroit's Conservatory of Music, locally known as Elma and Carl's House of Music. He remembers walking in to inquire about music lessons, and meeting a most remarkable woman.

Elma Hendricks, a talented musician who ran the struggling school with her husband, quickly developed a liking for the obviously talented youngster. "She became like my mom and even agreed to let me live with her and her family for a while," James fondly recalls.

"She took me under her wing and she tutored me in music. She was my vocal teacher, and she was my music teacher, and she taught me how to play the organ and piano. She even gave me free lessons."

That living arrangement, however, soon fell apart. "It was really tough because she was living with her father, and she hadn't really talked to her dad about bringing a young man in to live in the house. So I was only able to stay with her for a while."

Elma helped the sixteen-year-old obtain a room in a downtown YMCA, where James supported himself by working weekends at a record store that she and her husband operated as part of their business.

Still, James recalls feeling lonely and depressed. "It was a rough time of my life," he recollects. "And the relationship between me and my foster parents was getting uglier—it was all around just one big ugly situation."

To worsen matters, the teenager suffered an unexpected tragedy that increased his depression: a house fire in which three of his youngest siblings perished.

"You know, it's really strange, but I knew that was gonna happen," he states. "I dreamed one night that there were three white caskets by my bed. And Lord have mercy, that Saturday when I went to work I knew something had happened.

"My brother and uncle came down to the store, and soon as I saw them I immediately knew that something bad had happened. And they said there was a fire at the house, and the three youngest kids got burned up in the fire. The boiler in the basement had caught on fire and it blew up.

"And everybody, my mom and my brothers and my sisters, they were upstairs sleeping until my sisters smelled smoke. So they got hysterical and jumped out the windows. But three of them died from smoke inhalation—two girls and one boy."

James's powerful voice is tinged with sadness as he continues.

"My baby sister, Robin, she was six years old. David happened to be two, and little Marlin was one. And a child that my mother was baby-sitting also died in that fire. So it was a very tragic situation that my mother and I went through."

The following day, while sitting in church during the funeral service, James says that he came to a momentous decision, one that would affect the future of his life.

Instead of feeling angry at God for the loss he suffered, or denouncing his Maker for all the difficulties he had been experiencing over the years, the sixteen-year-old, instead, decided to embrace Jesus.

"I just remember I was sitting there at the church with my mom. It was a very tough situation for me. It was then that I decided to accept my calling into the ministry, to devote my life entirely to Jesus.

"All my life, even though I had always loved church, I had tried to do everything not to accept my calling to the ministry. I had run from it. But now I was no longer going to run from the Lord.

"It might look like God had forsaken me, but I thought it was God's way of getting my attention. You see, a lot of people don't understand that God permits certain things to happen just to get our attention. No, I wasn't going to hate God for what had just happened. I knew that this was His doing to get me going upward and upward."

James recalls how Elma patiently listened to him as he spoke about his desire to serve the Lord.

"James," she said, "there's somebody I want you to meet."

"Who?" he asked, wondering what his friend had in mind.

"Her name's Mattie Clark and she's the pastor of the Bailey Temple Church of God and Christ in downtown Detroit."

From the moment that he stepped foot into that church and met the charismatic pastor and gospel singer, James remembers falling under the woman's spell.

"When I walked out of the church that day I had gotten saved," he says in an emotion-filled voice. "I became a changed person. I gave my life to God. And I began to hang out with other young people who were saved and filled with the Holy Ghost, and that really helped me."

It was under the pastor's guidance that James not only began to flourish spiritually, but musically as well. The gospel music matriarch was well connected in music circles, and her sponsorship helped the talented teenager up the first few rungs of the ladder of success.

In 1974, James met someone else who was to have a profound influence in his life—the late gospel music star Rev. James Cleveland. James went on to attend Cleveland's Gospel Music Workshop of America in Chicago, where the twenty-year-old received the Thurston Frazier Scholarship Award and was discovered by a talent scout from Savoy Records.

That same year he recorded his first album, *I Thank You Master*, on the Savoy label. The record garnered moderate success. After three more recordings, James switched to the Malaco label, where his debut album, *Rev. Moore Live*, swiftly climbed to the top ten of both the *Billboard* and *Cashbox* gospel music charts.

In 1989, that album earned the young singer his first Stellar Award for Best Solo Performance and also an Excellence Award nomination from GMWA, the Gospel

Music Workshop of America. Next, James performed as a guest artist on the Mississippi Mass Choir's debut album, *Live in Jackson, Mississippi,* contributing to its massive success.

The disc stayed a record forty-eight weeks at Number One on *Billboard*'s Gospel Albums Chart, won four Stellar Awards, three GMWA Excellence Awards, and took three Dove nominations.

Grateful for his participation on their hugely successful debut album, members of the Mississippi Mass Choir agreed to perform as backup for James's next album. In March 1991, *Live With the Mississippi Mass Choir* became the nation's Number One gospel hit.

Now firmly entrenched as one of the top stars in the gospel music industry, James thought the hardships that for so many years had plagued him were things of the past. But, as he was soon to learn, his spiritual endurance would be tested even further.

"It was 1993 and I lost a close friend of mine, Frank Williams, who happened to be my mentor," James recalls. "He was a gospel singer and a producer. And he was the executive director for Malaco Records for its gospel division.

"He birthed my recording career," James unequivocally states. "He was a man who was a very low-profile brother. And he believed in me. He believed in me so much, and he wanted to see my career bloom, and it did bloom.

"It was because of him that I was blessed and fortunate enough to be one of the artists who sang on the Mississippi Mass Choir's first recording. But that year Frank passed on to be with the Lord."

Even today, James sounds mournful when he talks about the death of his best friend. Back then, however, James recollects that he nearly left the music business because of the sadness he felt.

"That really threw me for a loop because we were really close. He was like my brother, my big brother. He was somebody I could talk to about anything."

James relates one incident typical of how Frank would treat him: "I was having so many personal problems at the time that an executive at Malaco Records suggested that I needed to see a psychologist.

"And Frank was sitting there, and I felt so hurt because this executive was telling me I needed to see a psychologist. I was having financial problems and one problem after another. I wasn't a good manager with my finances. It was rough for me, because I never had anybody in my family to really help me."

James remembers how he left that meeting feeling embarrassed and humiliated. "Frank caught up with me after the meeting and he said, 'Listen, don't let him bother you.' I can't tell you how good that made me feel. That's the kind of guy he was.

"And when I made my mistakes, he would tell me where I was wrong. He would never put me down, but he would say, 'That was wrong. You need to straighten it out.' That's why when Frank died it was like something inside me died too. I just didn't feel like going on."

James recalls that he first learned of his friend's death while preparing to perform at the Baptist Center in Nashville, Tennessee. "I remember I was getting ready for the show and my manager, Debbie May, came into my hotel room with a young musician by the name of Jimmy White.

"She said, 'Sit down. How're you doin'?'

"I said, 'What's up, boss? What's wrong with you all? I've got to get ready for this concert.' They already knew that Frank had passed, and they just wanted to make sure I was all right. That's when they told me."

That was one moment in his life that the acclaimed gospel music star says he hopes never to have to experience again. "I've had some rough deals in my life, and I've gone through some bad experiences," he declares. "But his death really shook me. I couldn't believe it. I called Frank. I called his home. His pastor answered and he asked me how I was doing. I said, 'I'm fine, where's Frank?' "

The pastor switched the call to Frank's wife, which is when James remembers that the reality of the situation finally set in. "I said, Katrina, how are you doing, baby? How do you feel?

"And she said, 'As good as can be expected.' She said, 'Haven't you heard? Frank died today.' I immediately blacked out. My manager told me later that I was hollering 'It can't be true, it can't be true.' "

What happened over the course of the next week still remains pretty much of a blur for James. All he can recall is boarding a plane to Las Vegas in order to clear his head and try to escape the pain he was feeling.

But that pain refused to go away, clinging to him like a ghost. "I was refusing to go to Frank's funeral," he recollects. "I kept saying, 'I ain't going because he's not dead.' Well, they finally convinced me to get on the plane, and so I went to Jackson for the funeral. They allowed me to view the body by myself. And then I knew it was really true, that he was gone."

Although immersed in grief, James offers that he cannot recall one moment when he blamed God for the death of his friend. "No, I never lost my faith," he says with emphasis.

"I was just astonished. I was just overwhelmed. I mean, here was a man I had just talked to about three or four days ago, and he was telling me how excited he was about this new album we were going to do.

"No, I didn't lose my faith. I became stronger in my faith. The Bible says that all things work together for the good of them that love the Lord. I knew that God does things for reasons, and it's not for us to say, 'Well, why did you do that?' That's how I coped with it.

"I just believed that God knew what He was doing when he took Frank. And I didn't question God. I always tell people, 'Don't question the Lord and why He does things. It may be a blow, but He knows what He's doing. And sometimes, certain things like this can happen. God permits it to happen so that He can bring out the best in us.'"

James also recalls relying on prayer to get him through that ordeal. "I just kept saying, 'Lord, send your deliverance to me.' And He did. The only thing that was put in my spirit was to remember those times that I had with Frank that were good times."

A year later, James was to suffer another tragedy—an illness that to this very day threatens his life. Again, the artist whom many describe as the "King of Gospel Music" responded in a spirit-filled way.

His testimony begins in 1994 when James was ministering at a small church in Fayetteville, North Carolina. Still grieving for his friend, James had taken a temporary break from recording.

"It all started with me catching the flu. And I was in bed with the chills. And anytime you catch me in the bed from Sunday to Sunday and not in church, you know I've got to be sick. A month had passed, and I was getting weaker and weaker instead of better, so I asked the pastor's son to take me to the emergency room."

When the thirty-eight-year-old entertainer arrived at the local hospital, he was admitted complaining of chills and a serious nosebleed. After examining his patient, the doctor diagnosed James with the flu.

James remembers that the physician was about to dismiss him, when the doctor noticed an unusual swelling in his patient's ankles. "He was prescribing medicine for the flu when he looked down at my ankles," James recalls. "I was putting my clothes back on when he asked if he could run a few tests."

A half hour later the doctor returned with the test results in his hands.

"Reverend Moore, follow these nurses to your room. We've admitted you to the hospital," the doctor said.

"What?" James replied.

"I don't want you to wait a day more. Go."

"So they admitted me to the hospital. I had my vision at the time. I wasn't blind."

More tests followed, and then James was given the bad news. He learned that his kidneys had completely stopped functioning because of a high percentage of toxins in his bloodstream.

"The doctor said, 'Reverend, you have total renal failure, and also retinal deterioration.' He said that I had a lot of excess fluid in my legs—my feet looked like elephant feet—and that they were going to try and get the fluid out."

James, still reeling from shock, could not believe what he was hearing. He demanded to be released from the hospital. "I got so upset that I told the pastor's son to get me out of here. I had an IV in my arm."

"Listen, Reverend, we can't let you go," the nurse said.

"I said, 'Take this IV out, I'm going home. I don't understand why I'm going through this.'

"So I signed a paper and I went out on my own. I went into a state of denial. I didn't want to believe these things were happening to me, a thirty-eight-year-old man."

A month passed, and James remembers feeling worse than ever. There was one afternoon, while preparing to go onstage at the Church of God and Christ Annual Holy Convention in Memphis, Tennessee, that he could hardly find the strength to stand.

"I was sick and dying and I didn't even realize it," he submits. "Then I got a call from the president of Malaco Records, Mr. Tommy Count, Sr., who asked me to come to Jackson. Well, I was under the impression I was going there to finish editing my video. Little did I know that it was a plot to get me admitted to the hospital."

That day, as James stepped off the plane in Mississippi, he was greeted by several Malaco Records executives. "They told me that I'd been good to the company, and that they wanted to show how much they cared instead of letting me go this alone.

"They wanted their doctors to take a look at me. So I said, 'Okay, I don't have a problem with that.' What I didn't know was that they were going to send me to the hospital that very same day."

"When am I going?" James remembers asking his bosses.

"Right now," replied Stuart Madison, one of the record company's executives.

"Wait a minute, I can't go now," James protested. "It's a holiday."

Within the hour James found himself seated in the hospital emergency room. "I ended up going with Joyce Hans, who was the receptionist at Malaco. Mr. Madison had given her his American Express credit card to get me admitted."

After an examination, the doctors confirmed that the gospel star's kidneys had stopped functioning and that life-threatening toxins had entered his bloodstream. As a result, James was required to undergo dialysis three times a week to help cleanse him of these toxins, a procedure he must participate in to this very day.

"So they put me on dialysis and I didn't even know what dialysis was," he recollects. "I just couldn't believe what was happening to me. It was a frightening situation."

Things were to get even worse. James remembers returning to his room, where he was watching television. Suddenly, it felt as if all the lights had suddenly gone out.

"It was like my eyesight just went kaboom. It just left me. The eye specialist examined me and he told me I was legally blind." It was all too much for him, James recalls. "It tore me down. I cried and I cried. I just couldn't believe it. I just couldn't believe on top of everything else I was also going blind."

Severely depressed, James remembers how his spirits were lifted by the words of his new manager, Jerry Mannerly, words that gave him the courage to go on.

"He said, 'Listen, God can do anything. I know it hurts, but this ain't over.' And so I dealt with it. And every day the blindness got worse and worse, but I dealt with it."

If the accomplished singer's career was a phenomenon before, it now became what many describe as a miracle, as the gospel star fought back against the frailties of his body through an emphasis on his faith in God. Instead of anger, James felt strengthened by his ordeal.

"No, I didn't feel any anger toward God at all. In fact, it made me love Him even more. I felt like God was allowing these things to happen to see how much I really loved Him. And I know that He loves me. He confirmed His word to me. I once heard Him say to me, 'You're going to be a living testimony to Me.'

"And that's what I am. And I thank Him for that and I love Him more and more because He's a healer. He already brought me from death's door up until now— from death to life! These doctors had pretty much given up on me. This one doctor told me that my life was over. But God proved him wrong."

James remains convinced this all his bodily ills are only temporary, and that God will eventually heal him completely.

"Listen, I believe in God so much that I believe He will touch these eyes, which He is doing now, and touch my kidneys, which He is doing now. I know that He's a way maker. I know that He's a comfort keeper. I know sure as my name that God has delivered and touched my body, that He's refurbishing this body right now. I've got that kind of faith."

That conviction, he says, comes from having seen many examples of God's miracles at work over the years. "I have no choice but to believe in the Lord because of what I've witnessed Him do over the years.

"That's why I'll keep on shouting, singing, and preaching the praises of the Lord. In me, God has a warrior. I'm not going to be defeated by Satan and his henchmen. I've come out swinging."

Although he must still undergo dialysis treatments three times each week, James's poor physical condition has not slowed him down. Today, he is busy at work in the studio recording his latest album, while also preparing for his upcoming tenth-year anniversary celebration with Malaco Records.

In addition, the ordained minister and singer is touring the country as the star of *Why Good Girls Like Bad Boyz,* a gospel musical that last year opened in New York City's Beacon Theater.

"I'm having a wonderful time with this," he declares. "This is the first time that I've done any acting. I'm testing new ground."

As if that wouldn't tire out most healthy artists, James continues to perform before church audiences and concert crowds. He is also scheduled to be the guest artist at an upcoming national black pride convention sponsored by the Reverend Jesse Jackson.

There is also something else new in his life. The gospel star has recently become engaged, and soon plans to be married. "People tell me to slow down, that I'm trying to do too much," he says, smiling. "But my condition doesn't bother me when I'm doing something I love. And spreading the word of Jesus is something that I love doing."

If James is a living testimonial of how faith can overcome adversity, it is not a quality that he believes is exclusively his own. The inspired musical messenger humbly offers that anyone can surmount life's challenges by placing their full faith in the Lord.

"I say to people who are in a situation where they're going through surgery, or where their doctors have told them that they're not going to make it, to remember something.

"Don't give up because the doctor says it doesn't look good and that maybe you've only got six months to live—like they did to me. That's why I wrote the song 'It Ain't Over 'Til God Says It's Over.'

"Some of the doctors I've had were very arrogant. They thought they knew more than God. And they kept saying to me, 'Oh, no, oh, no!' But God has a way of doing things.

"So don't give up and throw your hands up. Because it could really be a test of God to see if you're going to really love Him and trust Him more than you trust the doctors."

As if to add emphasis to his words, the vocal powerhouse relates one final story about the miracle of faith. "There was this last situation a couple of months ago where I took sick. I was beginning to produce Brian Wilson's album, and I found out that a doctor had put a catheter that was not sterile in my chest."

As a result, James developed an infection that required hospitalization. "I was in the Jackson, Mississippi, Methodist Hospital for nearly a month," he states. "The infection had gotten into my bloodstream, and I couldn't even walk—I needed a wheelchair.

"The hospital called my mom and said, 'You'd better come to Jackson because we don't think he's gonna make it. But, of course, God again proved them wrong. God healed me. They thought I would never walk again. Now I walk on my cane and I'm doing well. This has made me trust Him even more.

"It ain't over 'til God says it's over," James joyfully proclaims. "And that's the way you gotta feel no matter what you're goin' through. Trust Him and believe in Him. Seek out God's face for what He can do for you. . . ."

KURT CARR

Photo by David E

Kurt is the youngest gospel star on the block. His experience in working with the late Reverend James Cleveland at a very young age catapulted him onto center stage.

As a result of that relationship, he went from performing as a soloist in various choirs to developing his own group, called the Kurt Carr Singers. It's a group that he handpicked based on many criteria.

He is so meticulous—and particular—about what he does and how he does it that Kurt has been called a perfectionist by people in the gospel music industry.

His latest album, which is the most successful project that he's ever done, has really taken him to another level. His writing ability, musicianship, and talents for arranging are going to continue to keep Kurt Carr in the forefront of the world of gospel music.

Look for him to be leading God's troops in the years to come!

As Kurt lay in a hospital room recovering from multiple stab wounds that he sustained while struggling with a carjacker, the last thing the Grammy Award nominee wanted to hear from his doctors was that he might lose the use of his hand as a result of his injuries.

But the Gospo Centric recording artist and three-time Stellar Award winner also remembers thinking that the Lord hadn't brought him this far along in his career to abandon him now.

The Connecticut native was supported in his conviction by a prophecy from the son of noted evangelist Oral Roberts, who told the injured musician that he foresaw a complete healing for him.

To his doctors' surprise, that prophecy came true. Today, the leader of the popular Kurt Carr Singers shares the story of his miraculous recovery whenever he feels the spirit of the Lord asking him to do so.

At such inspired moments, the grateful performer reminds his audiences that God can heal any open wound.

"There are so many people that have been physically, spiritually, and mentally cut," Kurt declares, "and many of them feel like an open wound. But people need to know that God can heal any kind of cut just as He completely healed me."

In talking about his life, Kurt does not allow his passionate devotion to Jesus to interfere with his delightful sense of humor.

What ends with a serious testimony about the healing power of God, begins with laughter as the versatile musician relates how, because of his close friendship with Jews as a youngster, he often wondered whether he might someday end up playing with a bar mitzvah band rather than performing before predominantly Christian audiences.

"All my schooling was private, predominantly Jewish schools," Kurt relates. "And all of my friends were Jewish. I probably went to about fourteen bar mitzvahs, and it's really amazing that I ended up playing gospel music."

Born and raised in Hartford, Connecticut ("I'm probably the first gospel artist ever to come from Connecticut"), Kurt recalls that his old neighborhood was a predominantly black and Hispanic one. Although he grew up on Hartford's mean streets, the gospel star recollects that he was able to avoid trouble.

"I was kind of quiet, kind of shy 'cause I was overweight. So I was a pretty good kid and I was by myself a lot," he explains. "I was an exceptionally gifted child, and my mother saw to it that I got into a special program for gifted children. So I went to some of the finest schools in Connecticut, and they all had strong music departments. I was very musical."

Kurt's mother, a keypunch programmer, and his father, who worked as a social worker, were not overly religious, he recalls. "My parents weren't regular churchgoers. We didn't go every Sunday.

"We went on Easter and Mother's Day, on special events. But at home we were taught about prayer, and about God and about Jesus and everything . . . and we said grace and our prayers at night. And they instilled a lot of moral lessons in us."

The middle one of three siblings—with an older brother and a younger sister—Kurt has fond memories of the occasions when he and his family would attend the Hopewell Baptist Church in Hartford, especially the music he heard played there. "There was something about the music that did something to me. There was something special about it," he asserts.

Thinking back, the singer and songwriter believes that his attraction to gospel music was one way in which "God moved through me. I believe I was called to do this—even before I was in my mother's womb I was called to do this. It just had to be. That's why that music attracted me.

"I mean, I didn't grow up around it; I didn't grow up hearing it; we didn't have any gospel records in my home. I told you, most of my friends, from kindergarten through high school, most of them were white or Jewish—mainly Jewish. That's why I'm so amazed at what I'm doing now—and why I know that I'm doing it because it's God's will for me."

Although he enjoyed church and the spiritual music he heard performed there, it wasn't until Kurt was thirteen that gospel music gripped his heart with real fervor.

"I remember that my mom went to New York to see a play. And she brought me back the sound track of *Your Arms Too Short to Box With God,* and a gospel record. It was Walter Hawkins's *Jesus Christ Is the Way.*"

It was a record that Kurt remembers being unable to put down. "I didn't really understand what was going on. But every day, for about a year, I listened to it."

"And then, eventually, I went back and got some of his earlier recordings. You know, I've worked with so many people, but I often say that his music is the reason that I'm doing what I'm doing today. I was anointed on that music. It was after that that I realized I wanted to get into the choir, and start singing and everything."

As fate would have it, at just about the same time Kurt was showing such deep interest in gospel music, his family relocated to a new house only a block from the Baptist church. The teenager couldn't have been happier.

"One Sunday I just told my mother that I wanted to go and join. And I went, and eventually I got in the choir. I had no real training, I really couldn't play the piano. I think I could probably play 'Chopsticks,' that's about all. I learned a little from my mother, who took piano lessons when she was a little girl."

He recalls one particular Sunday morning when the youth choir received the upsetting news that the choir's pianist was preparing to leave in order to attend college.

Soon afterward, while he was practicing "Chopsticks" during a choir rehearsal, the pianist approached the thirteen-year-old with a suggestion for him. "Wow, maybe I can get you to play for the choir while I go away to school," she said.

Kurt can still recall looking up and almost laughing. "I couldn't really play, so I thought it was very funny." The pianist, however, was dead serious. She went on to teach Kurt how to play one song before departing for college— "Satan, We're Gonna Tear Your Kingdom Down."

Today, widely known for his diverse approach to gospel music—employing everything from jazz and classical to hip-hop grooves in his compositions—Kurt laughingly relates how "the youth choir sang that song every time we had to sing for probably three to four months. I didn't know how to play anything else. But that kinda started me on my musical journey."

Two years later, it was a different story. Kurt was accepted into the church's older concert choir as a pianist. His acceptance into that group astounded him at the time.

"This was a really good choir," he relates. "They had played on some records in the early eighties with a gentleman named Benny Diggs. It just seemed unattainable that

I would ever be able to work with them, they were stars to me."

Yet another vacancy at the church helped to forge Kurt's career. "The minister of music left the church, and I went on to take his position. And I stayed there through college."

At the University of Connecticut, Kurt majored in music. He paid his way through college working in the school cafeteria and school library. "I went on a partial scholarship to that school, but I worked all these jobs to support myself," he relates.

After college, the talented young musician accepted a position as minister of music at Hartford's First Baptist Church of Connecticut, one of the state's largest black congregations. It was there that he formed the first incarnation of his current award-winning group, the Kurt Carr Singers.

It was also at this church that Kurt became more than just a Christian—he became a dedicated one. His memory of that day remains clear.

"We were singing on a program at Holy Trinity Church of God in Christ, which was pastored by a gentleman named Hubert Powell—he's also a gospel jazz musician. And it was after we finished singing that I really made a total commitment to Christ."

Trying to recapture that moment, Kurt recalls returning to his seat and suddenly being engulfed by a feeling he had never experienced before. "Yeah, I can still remember it clearly," he exclaims.

"It was an overwhelming feeling. I'd never been a smoker, or a drinker, and all that stuff, but I just had made the confession and the commitment to Christ."

The reaction from the church congregation as he did so was extraordinary, Kurt recollects. "The whole church shouted and carried on for at least an hour after that, because I was a public figure. People knew me.

"I was working at this church and I had a troupe. I was established. And it was a big thing in the city. I'm sure by the next morning, everybody knew. It was probably one of the greatest spiritual moments in my life."

On that day, Kurt recalls walking out of the church building feeling as if he were a completely different person. "I think it was then that I realized what I was called to do. This is when the pieces of the puzzle came together, and I realized that my whole life had changed. It was like my whole life was changing to serve the Lord."

His spiritual transformation also touched his family, the musician recalls. "My parents started coming to church, and my brother got involved in church. It kinda did draw my family to God."

Kurt's star began to climb in 1985. It was then, through an unusual sequence of events, that the young gospel artist met James Cleveland.

"That experience in church was my spiritual experience, but the turning point in my career—in really stepping out—was meeting James Cleveland," Kurt exclaims of his meeting with the departed minister.

Kurt remembers, however, that getting the minister's attention was no easy task.

"I had gone to his convention, the Gospel Music Workshop of America, three times, and each time I brought my group from Connecticut. I wanted him to hear us and discover us. And every time we sang he was either not there, or had just walked out of the room, or whatever. So he never got to hear us."

There was one year when Cleveland relocated his workshop from Florida to New York City. Because it was nearby, Kurt decided that he would attend. "I also decided not to bring the group, but just to go up there by myself."

Kurt's plan was to remain at the convention for just

one day, he relates. What he didn't figure on was the Lord having plans of His own for the gifted young artist.

"I had car trouble, so I ended up staying more than one day," he relates. "The next day I saw my friend Richard 'Mr. Clean' White, who's a singer and a preacher, and he was good friends with James Cleveland."

Kurt agreed to meet Richard for lunch, and as they were dining in a small restaurant located across the street from Madison Square Garden, who should walk in and join them—none other than the famous minister himself.

Kurt remembers being too nervous to even finish his meal. But what he gained as a result of that introduction was something even better than dessert; an invitation to walk across the street and audition for the gospel legend.

The legendary singer and evangelist became so impressed with the teenager's talent that he invited Kurt to move to Los Angeles and become his new music director.

"Richard had been telling him how well I played and everything, and finally James said, 'All right, let me hear you play something.' And I played.

"And, at the time, his musical director had submitted his resignation because he started to pastor a church. Before the week was over, I was offered the job. And by that January I had relocated to Los Angeles."

After traveling with the James Cleveland organization for four years, Kurt remembers beginning to feel restless. He wanted to do more for God with his musical gift.

"I got known as that 'little boy that can really play,' but I knew there was more for me to do," he relates. "So I thought about starting my own group." He got help in doing so from an unexpected source—Cleveland's daughter, LaShun.

"She could really sing, but she never really had the opportunity because her father was James Cleveland and that was a pretty hard act to follow," Kurt explains.

"So she never really developed her singing. And she and I kinda organized the group. And James supported us. In fact, we had our debut concert at his church."

Within a year, the six-member ensemble was already getting contract offers from various record companies. In 1991, Kurt and his group signed on the dotted line with Light Records.

"I guess that happened because I was known for my relationship with James Cleveland, and because we played at his conventions a lot and had lots of ability," he suggests.

Out of gratitude for everything that was going on in his life, the faith-driven gospel star decided to do something more for the Lord. Kurt took on the added responsibility of volunteer musical director for the seventeen-thousand-member West Angeles Church of God in Christ.

"It was another way of me giving back for all my blessings," he asserts. "I felt it was a true ministry because I wasn't doing it for money. When I go on the road with my group, it's kind of more a professional thing, where people buy tickets and everything. But this was volunteer work."

It was at the peak of his career that the versatile performer suffered a setback that nearly cost him his life. Kurt describes that incident as a "near death" experience that he believes was meant to be a test of his faith. He also proudly proclaims that he passed that test with flying colors.

"It was 1991 and we had just been nominated for two Stellar Awards," he testifies. "It was for my very first album on Light Records. I was twenty-nine years old at the time and I was returning home and I got carjacked.

"I had just bought a new car. And I had always thought if something like that happened to me, I would just say: 'Here, take it.' But I tried to resist and fight—I was struggling with this guy. And I actually got stabbed . . . one, two, three . . . five times."

Kurt pauses. "It's kind of hard for me to talk about it sometimes," he confides. "Sometimes you don't want to dredge up negative things that happen. But someone needs to know—to testify—how God heals cuts."

Continuing, the singer and songwriter remembers parking his car in the back of the Englewood, California, apartment building where he lived. "It was kind of a heavy drug area," he relates, "so, you know, there's this guy coming down the alley. And I'm thinking, I better not get out of the car until this guy goes by.

"Okay, so he walks past my car, and I'm fumbling, looking for my keys to open the garage. And as I get up out of the car, he puts a knife to my neck, and says, 'Gimme this car or I'll kill you.' He was on drugs or something."

Kurt still doesn't exactly know what got into him, but turning over his new car to this knife-wielding drug addict was not on his agenda. "Something in me just said, 'Try to fight'—something. And he had the knife and he was stabbing me. I didn't even realize I was being stabbed. I never thought that that was possible.

"And when I accidentally grabbed the knife, that's when I sliced my right hand, very severely. And my hands, you know, are my life. That's when I realized I had been stabbed. So I said: 'Just take it.' And he drove off with the car."

Bleeding profusely from his wounds, Kurt stumbled to a neighbor's door, where he cried out for help. "She let me in. I was drenched with blood. I didn't even realize I had been stabbed anywhere other than my hand. And she helped me and the ambulance came."

Lying in a hospital bed that following morning, Kurt remembers with horror how he had lost all feeling in his right hand. "There was numbness, and I couldn't move it. I had lost mobility from my right finger all the way to my thumb."

Meanwhile, word had spread among the hospital staff about the gospel singer who had been admitted suffering from knife wounds. "Some of the nurses and doctors were members of my church," Kurt relates. "And one of the doctors who belongs to my church came and told me that there was a strong possibility that I might never regain feeling in my hand."

Those words plummeted him into one of the darkest moments of his life, he recalls. *That* was the greatest test of my faith. And a lot of people don't even know about it," he exclaims.

"I was saying, 'Oh, my God, my life is over.' But that's when I realized just how strong my faith was. That fear passed and I never doubted that God was gonna heal me. I never doubted.

"I had been faithful to Him. I was serving Him. I was trying to walk in a certain way that He would want me to, and I just stood on that. And the doctors were saying: 'You know, we don't know. . . .' And I said, 'Well, *I* know.' "

One bit of news that cheered him up was that the police had found both his car and his attacker. "He had robbed a bank in my car, and they caught him. He went to jail for a long time. I was really glad about that."

In the weeks to come, Kurt was the recipient of even more good news: He began to be able to slightly move his injured right hand.

"I went through constant pain for about two months. And when I got out of the hospital, I didn't go back to that apartment. I stayed with friends for about four months."

Although his doctors still doubted whether the musician would ever be able to play again, Kurt recalls always believing otherwise. He was supported in his faith-driven conviction by one of his friends, Richard Roberts, son of the famous evangelist.

"Richard was at our church and he and his wife prophesied to me that I would play again," Kurt recalls. "And he laid hands on me and anointed me. He said I would not only play again, but use that very same hand."

He warmly remembers that there were many others who also prayed for his healing. "I had just begun working at the West Angeles Church of God when all this happened, and they prayed for me. They laid hands on me and anointed me with oil."

Slowly, miraculously, Kurt's hand began to heal. Eventually, against the odds, he found himself playing the piano again.

"I got back on my feet, and I've never looked back since," he proclaims joyously. "I was healed. I mean, I still have a very slight numbness in my thumb, but other than that I have complete mobility of my hand."

Kurt will not deny that despite all the faith he had that the Lord would heal him, he did entertain a few moments of doubt. "Of course, you know, the enemy tried to make me think that," he declares. "But I just rebuked him. I had to trust God, I had to. I didn't let anybody feel sorry for me and I didn't let myself feel sorry for me."

God was the only one he could really lean on, the recording artist recollects, because he was unable to tell his ailing mother what had happened to him. "She was three thousand miles away and always worrying about me.

"She had just had a heart attack. I knew that if I told her what happened it would've killed her. So I had to draw all my strength from God. I only had Him to depend on."

It is still sometimes painful for him to talk about that incident, but the acclaimed performer offers that he often feels moved by God to testify about the miracle he experienced back then.

Although Kurt is kept quite busy serving the Lord through his various ministries, the talented performer reveals that he hopes to go even further in his spiritual walk. He is giving serious thought to someday becoming an ordained minister.

"I believe that God is speaking to me, and giving me a word," he declares. "And I'm just waiting for His right time. If and when He calls me to be a minister and a preacher, I want my word—I want God's Word through me—to be as profound as my music."

Toward that end, Kurt relates that he studies Scripture whenever time permits. "Sometimes with all my traveling and with the church, I can't devote as much time to studying as I'd like to. I want to get to know His Word better."

It is his commitment to the Lord that also keeps him from accepting offers to perform on secular labels—although Kurt states that he does want to continue to expand his God-given musical talents.

"I remember James Cleveland once told me that my gospel music was too complex, because most gospel music is pretty basic and simple," Kurt recalls. "He said, 'People can't understand it; they gotta have something they can feel.' But I was trying to incorporate all my training in my music."

The fledgling artist paid attention to the advice he received, but remembers still feeling a bit restless about being locked into one kind of musical format.

"After I started the group and started making records, I started praying," he recalls. "I said: 'God, you've given me all of this education and knowledge, and I want to be able to use it.' "

Again, much to his amazement, Kurt is convinced that the Lord responded directly to his prayers. The talented musician soon found an outlet for his creativity that did not compromise his dedication to spirit.

"I started getting work doing television commercials. And that's been my way of letting the steam out. If I want to do something *real* jazzy, or real classical, or real New Age, or whatever, I do it through commercials."

To date, Kurt has done more than twenty national commercial voiceovers, various television theme songs, and several movie sound tracks. "My life is a testimony of faith," he fervently proclaims. "And with faith in God, opportunity has no measure and life has no boundaries."

The blessings that are part of his life are available to anyone if they follow a formula of prayer, fasting, and separation, the faith-driven gospel star attests. He goes on to explain:

"It's important to pray, to fast, and to separate yourself," he declares, emphasizing that separation is the most difficult discipline to master. "The years that I've been in California have been lonely years.

"But I had to separate myself from people, from things, so that I could really be with God. This is one way to really know Him. It's just like any relationship; you have to spend a lot of time with the person to get to know them."

Kurt is also a firm advocate of fasting. "It's important," he asserts. "I learned about fasting when I got saved at the Trinity Church of God in Christ. We had 'shut-ins,' where we'd go to church on Friday and come out Monday—no food, no toothpaste," he says with a laugh. "I don't fast as much as I should, but there's no better way to feel closer to God."

When it comes to praying, Kurt reveals that in his own life "one of the hardest prayers that I've learned to pray is 'Your will be done.' You know, it's hard not to always pray for things and, instead, pray that God's will be done.

"But I began to feel guilty praying all the time about things that I wanted: a new house, a new car, a big record, or whatever. And I've learned to just pray that His will be done.

"And I also spend a lot of time praying for other people. I pray for my friends. I pray for people like Walter Hawkins, and Tramaine, and all of those people. And Andrae Crouch and Donald Lawrence, who influenced my life. I even pray for people I don't really know and for the success of their ministry."

In his devotional moments, Kurt discloses that he approaches the Lord as if He were a close personal friend. "I know that God is a friend, and Jesus is our friend," he declares. "And I know that He loves like a father loves a child.

"And a good father is available for the child to come in any way that they need to if they need advice, or if they need just a friend—or even a light joking relationship. Jesus is all of that."

The mention of Walter Hawkins reminds Kurt of the gospel record that, as a youngster, played such an important role in his life. The accomplished singer adds that he has never forgotten the great debt he owes to the legendary gospel star.

"One of the most touching things that happened to me was my last record, where Walter Hawkins came and sat in the front row," he exclaims. "I got so choked up to think that this is the man whose music drew me, sitting here at my recording. And he's a minister, too. And he's called me several times and told me that my record is his favorite record of the year. And that's pretty awesome."

Besides his desire to become a licensed minister, Kurt offers that he looks forward to doing more producing. "I think my true gift is making other people be at their best," he explains. "I have some of the best singers in the country, and I've been blessed over and over again to get really great singers."

In addition, he is excited about his plans for a world tour to promote his new live album, *No One Else*. One destination he is eagerly looking forward to visiting is Africa. And with typical humility, he declares:

"It's just awesome that my ministry is going into the world. It's hard to believe, you know. It's hard to believe where the Lord is leading me. But when God gives you the gift of song, you can go anywhere so He can be heard."

HEZEKIAH WALKER

Photo by Norman Roy

Hezekiah is a special deliverer of the Word, whether it's through his writing, singing, or straight-up preaching—which, by the way, he does very much like a seasoned minister of many years.

I marvel at how God uses Hezekiah to excite the crowds to respond to his powerful messages.

In my opinion, Hezekiah has one of the most powerful choirs since the Thompson Community Singers from Chicago, Illinois. The choir is well rehearsed, disciplined, and sincere when they come to give the Word. As he matures in years, he matures in understanding and outreach.

Hezekiah also has a flare for fashion, which I like. He loves to establish that East Coast sound, which is "thumping on the four." I expect him to continue his great choir presentation for years to come, and also to expand his preaching ministry and eventually settle down to a committed congregation.

His testimony concerning his struggles gives evidence that he is touched by God.

One of today's top gospel stars, Grammy Award winner Hezekiah Walker knows what it's like living in a world that seems to be reeling out of control.

The singer and pastor was reared in that kind of world—Brooklyn's rough-and-tumble Fort Greene neighborhood—where violence and crime swirled all around him.

But unlike many of his friends, Hezekiah found a way out. He developed an understanding that God had more important plans for him than hanging out with a tough bunch and possibly ending up in a body bag.

And, today, the 1998 Grammy nominee celebrates his victory through his new and fresh gospel music sound and his work as pastor of Brooklyn's Love Fellowship Church.

"When I look back over my life and see where God has brought me from, it's impossible not to feel confident and trusting in Him," the thirty-five-year-old gospel artist proclaims. "The Lord lifted me up and turned me around."

Turning back the pages to the days when he was "a poor boy growing up in a housing project," Hezekiah says he fully understands many of the hardships and challenges that today's inner-city youngsters face.

After all, he once faced those same challenges. And the acclaimed gospel music star asserts that he still carries those memories like scars. He recalls trying to survive in the violent world of the projects—where gun-toting youth gangs, drugs, and other vices were a constant way of life.

"I never really got into that kind of stuff, but I was surrounded by it all the time," he attests. "I did the basic normal hanging out on the street corner—you know, the party type."

Hezekiah praises God, his love of music, and, mostly, his mother's strong hand for keeping him in school and church—and out of trouble. "I don't remember my dad too much. He died when I was fourteen. And I don't remember him being very religious."

His mother, however, was a different story.

"She would take me and my younger brother and two sisters to church. And that experience stayed with me. It stayed in my heart. I believe it was my mother's faith that kept me from getting out of control."

Religious services at the Greater Bibleway Church in nearby Crown Heights were a weekly event that Hezekiah still recalls with pleasure. "I enjoyed the singing; I enjoyed the preaching. That church had so much charisma, and it was full of young people."

Hezekiah's natural musical ability was on display at an early age. He began singing in church when he was eight years old, and remembers being held spellbound by the gospel music he listened to.

"I'd always be fascinated at church when I would see people sing gospel music," he recollects. "I'd see the response of the people, the enlightenment, and how they were really touched by the music."

Although away from home the youngster also listened to other kinds of music, the award-winning performer recalls that gospel always held a special place in his heart.

"There was just a difference about it. It was the kind of music I wanted to sing," he declares.

"I wanted to be able to sing and touch people's hearts and see the emotions on their faces. So I made up my mind as a child that this was the kind of music I wanted to sing, because I wanted people to react like that."

He continued to hone his singing skills throughout most of his teenage years by performing at churches and elsewhere throughout the New York City area. And in 1985, shortly after his twenty-first birthday, Hezekiah took a major step toward establishing his professional career.

He formed the first incarnation of his Love Fellowship Crusade Choir with only twelve singers. Since then, the award-winning choir has grown to well over one hundred members, with records that consistently top the gospel charts and appearances at Madison Square Garden and Carnegie Hall.

Hezekiah smiles mischievously when asked about why he formed the choir. "I don't really want to go into detail about that," he replies. "Let's just say that a discrepancy arose, and me and some of the other members were asked to leave a community choir that I belonged to."

Undaunted by his dismissal, Hezekiah gathered his fellow outcasts and, along with some other friends, began building a choir of his own. He recalls that it didn't take long for word to spread about the new choir's remarkable singing ability, and its unusual "urban-style" gospel music.

Although Hezekiah and his popular choir were being kept quite busy, he remembers how life on the streets seemed to lure him. "I guess growing up you go through different stages in life," he reflects.

"I know in high school I went through peer pressure— you know, pressure from my friends who weren't involved in church. It seemed like they were just having a good time while I had to go to church.

"So I kind of struggled with that. It was a test of my faith. I didn't completely leave the church, but I tried to hang out a little bit. And then I realized it wasn't going to work for me."

What changed his mind is what Hezekiah saw going down on the streets. "I really figured it out that this kind of lifestyle was not for me, that it was destroying all my friends," he declares. "The drugs and shootings were killing all my people.

"I looked around and saw everyone doing drugs. I saw friends getting shot. When I was younger hanging out, everything we used to do was real clean. But then it became dirty. So I said, 'No, this ain't for me.'

"I also just felt that I had, from early childhood, this special touch by God to really sing, and that I should be using my talents to help people. And what better way was there to help people than through gospel music?"

It was a decision that the versatile vocalist states he has never regretted. "I mean, it was the best move I'd ever made in my life. I laid a strong foundation for my future. And as a result of that foundation I've never been happier than I am today."

There is another perhaps even more important reason why Hezekiah ultimately rejected the street life. At age twelve, he had already devoted himself to the Lord.

"You know, I can still remember the actual time when that happened. I was sitting in church—at least going through the routine of going to church—because all my friends were there and I enjoyed the singing and I enjoyed the fellowship.

"But it wasn't real to me. When it became real to me was on that Sunday. I remember that I was just sitting in church, and I really decided to pay attention to the preaching. And that day, you know, I just had a special touch from God."

Hezekiah pauses as he tries to recapture his feelings at the time. "It was like, you know . . . like an innermost feeling. I felt, like . . . this is it—this is the place for me forever. That same day I was baptized and saved."

Upon leaving the church that morning, the faith-driven gospel star remembers feeling as if he had shed his old skin. "My friends and my family all noticed the change in me," he relates.

"And that's when I pretty much stopped hanging out and dedicated my life to the church. Then later I was tempted a little to hang out again, but it still wasn't for me."

Hezekiah can only shrug his shoulders when asked why he believes he was touched by God. "I just think that I was rewarded because of my mother's faith in Him," he offers. "Out of the hundreds of young people that grew up in the Fort Greene area, I really think I was singled out because of that."

A note of sorrow enters the gospel star's voice when he talks about his mother. "I was only twenty-one years old when I lost her," he says softly. "She was my stability, my inspiration, and my anchor.

"It's like God transferred her spirit to me. She paved the way through her faithfulness for me to do this. That's why I was singled out. I was special to God because my mother was special to Him."

Although he is today one of gospel music's most sought-after performers, Hezekiah notes that his success did not come without some serious challenges to his faith. "Basically, when I first started out singing I was just singing locally here, just in the area," he relates.

"And you know, after singing for a few years it seemed like I wasn't going anywhere. It seemed repetitious. I was singing for at least eight or nine years all over New York City, and I wasn't taking off.

"Yeah, it was depressing. I was singing by myself to small groups and I felt I just had to keep doing that if things were someday gonna happen. It was a real test of my faith, but my faith was strong.

"I think I kept my faith because that's all I had. If I had something else I probably would have leaned on that. But all I had was my faith and it got me through that time."

It was 1985, shortly after he had formed his first choir, that Hezekiah believes his faith finally began to be rewarded. His fledgling Love Fellowship Choir signed with Sweet Rain Records, a small Philadelphia-based label.

The choir's first album became so popular that the company could not keep up with the orders. Two more albums followed with similar results.

In 1991, Hezekiah and his choir switched to the larger Benson Records label in Nashville. That resulted in a quick rise to the top of the gospel charts for the singer and his choir. In 1995, the choir's *Live in Atlanta at Morehouse College* album earned it a Grammy Award.

Reflecting on all his past success, the poor boy who grew up in a violent Brooklyn housing project humbly submits that he has been blessed by God. "That's why when, today, I look back over my life and see where God has brought me from, it's impossible not to feel confident and trusting in Him," he declares.

One way that Hezekiah tries to give back for all his blessings is through his church ministry. As pastor of the Love Fellowship Church in the Brooklyn neighborhood where he and his wife, Monique, and their young daughter, KiAsia, live, the acclaimed gospel star is always seeking ways to help troubled youngsters.

"I'm glad we're able to reach people, especially young people," he proclaims. "I understand them 'cause I've faced many of their hardships and challenges.

"And I want them to realize that the church is more than I ever thought it was when I was their age. It's more than we were taught it was. I want to really get them into it, so that they can really enjoy it. I want them to enjoy more than just the singing."

Hezekiah discloses that he first accepted his "call" to the ministry at age eighteen, and for many years served as pastor to his choir. But, he adds, it never felt that he was doing enough to serve God.

"I was doing that and bringing the word of Jesus to millions of people through my musical ministry, but I ran away from actual preaching—I tried to get away from it."

That changed in 1993, when the gospel music star decided to found his own church. Hezekiah laughingly recalls that things did not get off on the best footing.

Although he was the pastor of a choir with more than one hundred members, the gospel artist and minister relates that most of his singers belonged to their own home churches. "So there I was on that first day preaching to about twelve people."

Today, however, the Love Fellowship Tabernacle Church is flourishing, with a congregation of more than a thousand worshippers. "God has blessed us," he declares. "We're looking for another building now, because we can't even hold the members we have.

"I'm looking forward in the near future to having one of the strongest churches here in New York City. I'm also looking forward to doing some work over in Africa."

Another ministry that Hezekiah is quite proud of is his outreach to the homeless. "Being a pastor has enhanced my career as a gospel singer," he asserts.

"Preaching and having to feed hungry people each week have given me new insights into my studies. And in studying I've learned much more about gospel music and why it's important. I learned that it's much more than I ever realized it was."

For those seeking to strengthen their walk with the Lord, Hezekiah counsels keeping one's thoughts and prayers focused on the Almighty. "God requires a lot of prayer time," he declares. "It's through prayer that you can be touched by Him. Anybody who is willing to spend time in prayer can be touched by God."

The singer, songwriter, and pastor discloses that prayer is something he does much of. "There are times when I just pray continuously," he explains. "And I'll pray just about anywhere and at anytime—in my car, while I'm walking, before I go onstage."

Looking ahead, Hezekiah hopes that in the years to come he will be able to reach an even wider audience for the Lord through his music.

With that goal in mind, Hezekiah, known as an innovator and updater of gospel music who has brought a fresh new sound to the genre, keeps on searching for new ways to bring Jesus' message across to his audiences.

What he is looking for, the acclaimed performer explains, is a format that will have an appeal to all God's people. "I study secular music and artists to try and understand what it is about that music that attracts millions of people—especially young people," he adds.

He candidly admits that secular radio has influenced him—especially such stars as Michael Jackson, Jodeci, and Boyz II Men. "I'm incorporating traditional and contemporary gospel into my material, hip-hop, R&B, pop—it's all there," he declares with emphasis.

"I want to try to incorporate that same excitement into gospel music and what we're trying to do for the Lord— as long as it's done from the heart and in Jesus' name.

"If Jesus is in the music, how can it be wrong? My mission is to lift up the name of Jesus, to build a foundation in praise so that God can be lifted, and also to add a taste of entertainment."

Hezekiah, however, does caution against an artist becoming too immersed in the form rather than substance of gospel music.

"Sometimes gospel singers—especially some of the groups—they get too caught up in entertaining," he contends. "They get lost in it. You have to know when to come in and preach.

"You can't take the music to an extreme. You have to put the message and the music all together and make it work. That's what I try to do. I use a contemporary sound and I use it to wake up the world to Jesus."

LASHUN PACE

Photo by Glamour Shots

This is one incredible woman! The Pace Sisters and LaShun have a musical blend that is unmatched. You usually find that among siblings who sing together. They certainly carry on that tradition of matched harmonies that sisters excel at.

LaShun stands out as one of the leading female vocalists in the gospel music industry. I think her Mahalia Jackson persona is going to catapult her into the year 2000 in a unique way.

First of all, LaShun has a most unusual testimony because of her marital experiences, which she so openly talks about. Through those experiences this talented singer indicates that she has been touched by God, elevated from her dire position of sadness and depression.

She speaks very candidly and openly about how the Lord helped to get her as far as she is, and her testimony is quite an inspiring one. With her abilities and stick-to-it way of doing things, LaShun will continue to reign as one of gospel music's favorite female vocalists.

God bless this very special soldier in God's army!

$\mathcal{B}$eneath LaShun Pace's glamorous public persona as a successful gospel music star exists a dark tapestry of memories about a painful period in her life when, sorely depressed about the failure of her marriage, she tried to kill herself while pregnant with her second child.

But there is another, more positive memory as well—of a sudden, exalting moment in the midst of that despair when the Georgia native felt the Lord's presence. At that moment, all thoughts of suicide and feelings of rancor toward her husband suddenly vanished from her mind.

Today, the thirty-five-year-old Stellar-winning gospel diva devotes much of her time to sharing her testimony with others who are gripped by despair.

"Don't give up your faith if you're struggling with something," the Savoy Records star counsels. "The Lord can see you through anything. Keep the fight going—just keep going. Remember, all help comes from the Lord."

LaShun's unswerving devotion to the message of the Lord has its beginning in the Pool Creek neighborhood of Atlanta, where she was reared. "It was a neighborhood in the southeast part of the city, and we grew up right by the main post office—we called it the Big White House," she recalls.

The versatile singer and actress, who appeared in the hit movie *Leap of Faith* starring comedian Steve Martin, portrays her family as being "kind of in between" poor and middle class. "There were nine girls and three boys growing up in a one-bedroom house. I was the fifth child."

She can still recall going to the grocery store for her mother and "asking the man if I could get food on credit, because none of my other sisters would do it." Most of the time, those groceries were paid for with food stamps, LaShun recollects.

LaShun's father, who had carpentry skills, mostly worked as a handyman, while her mother "cleaned white people's homes" and, later, worked as a school custodian.

The relationship between mother and daughter was a very close one, LaShun offers.

"I would go everywhere with my mom, helping her. When she took sick I took her job and cleaned for her. I was doing all this from the age of eleven until I was twenty. I would go with her to clean the white people's homes—and I don't mean to be negative when I say that.

"I had no idea why I was going with her, but as the years progressed and she got sick, I would take over for her. I was there and I knew what to do and these white folks enjoyed my work. And I also started cleaning the schools for her—it was another job that she had. It was hard labor. I sometimes had to clean three buildings in one day."

Reflecting back on those days, LaShun honestly admits that had anyone back then told her she would someday set the pace for gospel achievement, she would have looked at them as if they were crazy.

Yet there was one person who did, indeed, exactly that—and LaShun never laughed at him. It was gospel's noted Rev. Clay Evans, who prophesied that the talented young woman would eventually pick up and carry the torch left by the mother of gospel music, Mahalia Jackson.

"I had no inkling that I would be a recording artist where I am today and doing things that I'm doing today—especially that movie with Steve Martin," she declares.

"I really had no idea that I would do those things because I was a shy singer. I'd never be out front, and I'd let everyone else I sang with do the leading. I wasn't even aware of my range until after high school."

Raised in a devoutly Christian household where both her parents were musically inclined—they sang with quartets and in the church choir—LaShun says music has been important to the family for generations.

"My grandparents on both sides used to sing. And my grandfather used to do note singing, which we call now *a cappella,*" she relates. "My grandmother and great-great-grandmother, they also sang.

"My daddy sings, and my mom sings. We all used to sing in church all the time. When we came out of her, the first thing we did was come to church and sing," she says with a laugh. "So I come from a long line of people who sang."

The gifted artist fondly recalls how impressed she always was by her musically gifted parents. "My mom used to sing with the church choir, and then the state had a choir that she sang with.

"I'd be in the audience and listen to her sing. And my dad sang with a quartet group. They both traveled across the country. And I was so proud of both of them. I wanted to be like them."

Religion also factored heavily into her family life. "We had a very strict religious upbringing," she declares. "We were members of the Church of God in Christ, so we couldn't listen to any R&B whatever, no jazz. Everybody thinks that since I do a little jazz I used to listen to it. But I never listened to it in my life.

"And we couldn't go to games that the school had, and no dances. When we were in elementary school we were at one talent show—I think I was eight years old—

and we won that. And we couldn't date any boys and we couldn't be on the phone longer than fifteen minutes."

Recalling those days evokes a chuckle in her voice. "And when a guy would come over to the house, we had this nice long antique sofa, and it had three pillows. The guy had to sit on one end, and we had to sit on the other end. We couldn't hold hands. It was a very strict home."

There was one time when LaShun rebelled against such strict rules, and paid a painful price for it, she laughingly recollects. "I remember that I slipped my little radio under the pillow at night, and when I woke up there was a belt on my behind. It was my father yelling at me, 'I told you not to listen to that devil music.'"

She relates another incident where disobeying her parents' rules got her into lots of hot water. "I remember that my mom let us go to one party that the music teacher was having. She begged my mom, 'Please, this is the end of school and I think I'm leaving.' So my mom let us go."

What the youngster did not realize was that the Kool-Aid at the party had been secretly spiked with alcohol by her mischievous classmates. "My teacher had promised my mom that there wouldn't be any drinking or nothin'. So me and my sisters didn't know they had spiked the Kool-Aid.

"And I got one of those Dixie cups and this guy came around and said, 'LaShun, this is gonna be the best Kool-Aid you ever had.' And I drank some of that and I was sittin' in a chair just laughin' at everybody that walked by. And I really had nothin' to laugh at."

LaShun had nothing to laugh at, either, when her mother found out what had happened. "Oh, did I get a scolding," she says, smiling. "That was the kind of environment I grew up in."

In the 1970s, while still in high school, LaShun and her eight equally talented sisters decided to put their remarkable voices to good use. They formed a group, calling themselves The Anointed Pace Sisters.

From the moment they began appearing together, the sisters enthralled audiences with their singing. They even went on to win the Best Gospel Group award at the Annual Church of God in Christ Music Convention, then under the direction of the late evangelist and gospel music matriarch, Dr. Mattie Moss Clark.

LaShun and her sisters further developed their singing and ministering abilities when they began working and traveling with the Rev. Gene Martin and the Action Revival Team in the late seventies.

But it was Dr. Clark who, LaShun remembers, encouraged her to expand her vocal talents as a solo artist. "She used to come to lead our conventions a lot and listen to us sing—her daughter is one of the famous Clark Sisters. And I enjoyed singing under her leadership and so I knew I wanted to sing.

"But when she suggested that I go solo, I really didn't want to do it until my sisters had put out our first album. So I waited until they had put out two albums," says the entertainer whose voice has been described as "one of the nation's natural resources."

When in the 1980s the nine lively, fun-filled sisters attained national recognition with their debut album on Savoy Records, *U Know,* which quickly climbed to the top of the gospel charts and remained there for more than a year, LaShun, then twenty-six, believed it was now time for her to make a career change.

Her first big break came in 1988, when she recorded the song, "In the House of the Lord," with Dr. Jonathan Greer and the Cathedral of Faith Choir. The choir's label, Savoy Records, acknowledged LaShun's enormous contribution to that effort by signing her to a recording contract of her own.

Two years later, in 1990, LaShun recorded her debut solo album, *He Lives,* which gained national attention when it shot up to number two on *Billboard*'s gospel charts and remained in the top twenty for more than a year.

The album was so successful that there was even mention of LaShun being dubbed the next "queen" of gospel music. In her thirties, with her star on the rise, the young gospel artist felt like she was sitting on top of the world.

For LaShun, it was all the fulfillment of a vision that had been presented to her by the Rev. Clay Evans, a minister noted for his special gift of prophecy. What the minister had not foreseen was the trial she would have to endure at this very juncture in her life.

Then in her second marriage and pregnant with her second daughter, Aarion, serious cracks began to develop in the marital relationship.

Even today, LaShun is hesitant to reveal the specific reasons for the breakup of her eight-year marriage, other than to say that "I knew that my mind was ready to snap from the things that were happening to me. And I was close to having a stroke. But going through that I saw God bring me through."

LaShun's voice still is tinged with sadness as she relates what she considers one of the worst moments in her life. "Some of the things Edward was doing during our marriage were taking my respect away from him," she asserts without further comment.

"And I was just so tired of so much stuff, that I was saying to myself, 'God, I'm pregnant and it don't seem that he can even respect that. I can't go through this anymore.'

"Things between my husband and myself were getting so bad that I just knew I had to leave him. There was even a time when I thought he was going to hit me. And my sister was living with me at that time. You could see my dress shaking on my stomach—that's how nervous I was."

She pauses, still hurt by that painful memory. "There was a decision that had to be made and for better or for worse I made it. He didn't want to leave me. But I was raised that if something is bad you try to make it good. And if things don't work out, then you just face that reality.

"I mean I loved Edward. He enhanced me. He helped my career. He took me to different things to meet people, and he was a wonderful business manager. But there were other things plaguing him that Edward needed to deal with. I have no regret marrying Edward, but I do regret the divorce that we went through."

LaShun is not proud of saying it, but she can recall being so hurt over the breakup of her marriage that she became angry with the Lord. "I remember being so depressed that I didn't even want God's help. I was angry at Him.

"I had grown up a virtuous woman—I had never been with a man except the two that I had married—and I was angry that this was happening to me. I was doing that whole blaming thing. And I went into a deep depression. It was so bad that I wanted to kill myself while I was carrying my baby."

Even now, LaShun says it still seems almost incomprehensible to her that she had once even considered doing so. But that was exactly what she was thinking about at that point in her marriage, she admits.

"I remember I was sitting in the living room and I was looking out the window. It was a beautiful day, and I was thinking, 'I can't go on anymore.' I had never thought about suicide before, but I just wanted to end it. I remember thinking, 'Please, just let them find me in time to save my baby.'"

LaShun got up from the couch and, almost in a daze, slowly walked to the bathroom. There was something there that she knew would once and for all put an end to all her suffering—a knife!

"We purposely kept that knife in the bathroom so that my oldest daughter, Xenia, couldn't find it, because it was super sharp," she explains. "So I knew where it was. I got up and went into the bathroom, but I couldn't find that knife anywhere.

"I kept thinking, 'Where is it? I know it's here somewhere.' And I kept thinking, 'You know, God, I can't go on any more.' I never thought about this before, but I just wanted to end it."

What happened next is like fragments of memories in her mind. LaShun can recall her husband furiously banging on the bathroom door and shouting out her name. She also remembers how all that pounding on the door frightened her even further.

"The banging didn't make things any better for me. My nerves were shot and he's trying to kick down the door. What I didn't know is that he had put the knife somewhere else.

"So he kicked the door in and he came in and he said, 'What's the problem?' I couldn't talk. I was just filled with tears, and I ran out of the house and around the back."

It was then, LaShun testifies, in the midst of one of the most terrifying moments of her life, that she experienced a miracle that would forever change her.

Now there is a mixture of joy and awe as she relates her testimony. "I was standing behind the house—no one inside knew where I was—and it was like peace just came over me. I was looking at this big, beautiful tree and the sun was just beaming on my face.

"It was like the sky had opened up. The sun got brighter than I had ever seen it. And, I kid you not, it was like the heavens had suddenly opened up. And I heard God saying, 'You will never suffer this way again.' I know I heard Him say that." She repeats the statement: "You will never suffer this way again."

"You know, I just can't describe it. There are so many movies out there about women being abused. But if I could see that particular scene in a movie, it would really touch me. It was just so awesome."

Suddenly, all the fear and anxiety she had been feeling were gone, LaShun recalls. Calmly returning to the house, she remembers having "this nice warm feeling that was all over me."

As her husband and sister looked on wordlessly, LaShun silently packed her clothes in a suitcase. "One of my cousins showed up and I went on to my mom's house, and I never heard from Edward again."

LaShun remembers that as the car sped away from the house, she turned around for a final glance. It was then that she experienced a second miraculous moment: In her heart she no longer felt any hatred or bitterness toward her husband.

"God had healed me from bitterness," she proclaims. "I was literally hating Edward, and the hatred started when I was in the marriage. I just wanted out, freedom from what was going on. But now that state of mind was gone. God brought me through this. I saw God literally help me and bring me peace of mind. He had touched me."

In the weeks that followed, the gospel singer recalls feeling God's presence in her life on one more occasion— and she believes it kept her from dying.

"I had moved in with my mom and dad by this time," she recollects. "And they had moved out of their bedroom—they gave me their bedroom. I knew my parents loved me, but when they did that . . . My dad was even sleeping on the sofa.

"I remember I was sitting in the rocking chair—I'll never forget it. And I felt like something was crawling through my hands. And I knew we didn't have bugs. So I ran to my mother and I said, 'Mother, I feel like something is happenin' . . . I feel like somethin' is going through my hands.'"

To this day, LaShun says she will never forget the concerned expression on her mother's face. "She took one look at my mouth, and my mouth was twitching from one side to the other side.

"She said, 'You're getting ready to have a stroke. Whatever it is, you need to let it go and give it to God, because you don't need to have a stroke carrying a baby.'"

Falling down on her knees, LaShun prayed to the Lord. "I said, 'God, please, don't let me have a stroke.' And I just sat in a chair because I couldn't lie down.

"And God just touched me . . . and those feelings in my hands just left. It was the second time He had saved me in a month. It was miraculous, incredible! So much had happened back to back that I just can't tell you everything."

Although she was twice touched by God, LaShun rue-fully recollects still not being entirely grateful for such blessings. Today, she believes that much of her ingratitude stemmed from the feelings of depression that were weigh-ing her down, even after giving birth to a healthy new daughter.

"I remember one day when my baby was only two days old I looked at her—she was on the bed—and I just broke into tears. I was about to lose it. I was saying to myself, 'How am I going to support this baby?' And I was still feeling some anger toward God.

"My godparents were there when this happened, when I broke. But my godfather laid hands on me and immedi-ately started praying. I was yelling, 'I hate Him, I hate Him, why did He do this to me?' "

Gently consoling her, LaShun remembers her god-father telling her: "That's the wrong spirit, LaShun. He died and went to heaven for you."

Those words brought tears to her eyes, she remem-bers. It was at that moment that the gospel star vowed never again to question God's purpose in her life, a promise she has tried to keep to this very day.

"About a week after that I was on the road working, trying to bring a little money in. And it was happening. He was helping me. To see God now bringing me through all of this, I just can't really explain how I felt."

LaShun halts to wipe away tears. "I'm crying now, and I'm not trying to talk sadness, or anything. But I really saw God as God. You know, growing up as a little girl, seeing my mama, testifying—I grew up on all that—but it wasn't really real to me.

"But having been through this stuff, now I knew God was real. Man, it was mind-boggling. I thought I knew God when I was married—you know what I'm sayin'. But I hadn't even scratched the surface.

"Now I could say with confidence that I trusted Him with my life. I knew God loved me, and I no longer felt depressed. I came to know Him in another way. And I've been on a wonderful spiritual trip since then."

Trying to understand why she has been so touched by God, LaShun offers that it is because of the way she always cared for her parents. "I always took care of my mom—and my daddy—when I was growing up," she explains.

"Even before she took ill I took good care of her. And my daddy, too. I can still hear my daddy saying, 'Lord, I sure wish I had a glass of water.' I was up. I was always the first one of anybody to jump up and get whatever my daddy or mother wanted."

There is another reason why LaShun believes this explanation to be true. She submits that God told her that was the case.

"I know that's the reason because the Lord told me that in Chicago in a hotel room. I heard His voice, and He said, 'You know why you're so blessed?' And I started naming all this stuff. And He said, 'No, because you were so blessed to your mother.' And I started crying again, and I was saying, 'Oh, God, thank You.'"

Although LaShun has become one of gospel's most popular and sought-after recording artists—picking up three Grammy nominations, and an armful of other awards along the way—she does admit to sometimes still feeling impatient about the progress of her career.

At such moments, LaShun confides that she can become her own worst critic. "There are things I want—more engagements, more money like some of these other artists are making. I still don't have a house for myself and my daughters. I'm living with my sister. I don't even own my own car.

"I'll say, 'Lord I'm trying to live right, but it just ain't happening for me. I know I ain't perfect, Lord, but I ain't done nothing wrong, and da, da, da, da, da. And I'm just sick of it.'

"I remember once I called my mother and told her, 'I don't feel it. God ain't done this for me. I've been trying to live faithfully all these years and it ain't happenin'.' "

To banish such doubts, the versatile vocalist says she focuses on all the blessings the Lord has brought into her life, and also offers up prayers. "I'll even call my mother and ask her to pray for me at those moments. And I always come back to the Lord."

Although a devoutly committed Christian, and an active member in the Church of God in Christ, LaShun, like many other gospel artists, admits to having been tempted over the years by recording deals from the secular music industry.

Most recently, LaShun had an opportunity to perform on the sound track of the hit 1996 hit film *The Preacher's Wife*, giving her worldwide exposure—an offer she ultimately declined.

"My talent is a gift from God and I intend to use it for God's purpose only," she proclaims. "There's a lot of pressure on gospel artists to sing secular music. But I refuse to do that."

Today, another way in which LaShun dedicates herself to the Lord is by sharing her testimony with her audiences. By doing so, she hopes to encourage them to keep their faith no matter what is troubling them.

"I'm not a traveling evangelist, but I feel that God has called me into the ministry," she declares. "I tell people wherever I go that I'm not their ordinary gospel singer.

"I say, 'I don't just give you songs and let you go.' I

have to minister, and the ministering comes from things that I've encountered, the experiences that I've gone through."

What pleases LaShun the most at such moments is when she feels as if she has touched someone's heart. "The Holy Ghost will tell me to talk about this or that, and, afterward, different women come to me crying that they were in the same situation. They say, 'Just by giving your testimony, it helped me.' "

She also encourages prayer, which fills much of her own life. "Ever since I was twelve years old, I'd get up between two and three o'clock in the morning to do my praying. It never fails. All my life I've done this, and I still do.

"I talk to the Holy Ghost. I pray for me and my children, and I pray for people abroad. I pray that God keeps me anointed and humble and that He keeps me from the enemy . . . because the devil is so tricky.

"My mom one time taught us all to pray, 'Lord, keep us one step ahead of the enemy.' And I pray for Israel and Jerusalem and I pray for the leadership of that country. It's nothing long and drawn out, I just pray to Him the way I'm talking to you now."

She has simple advice for anyone wishing to intensify their spiritual experience: Read the Scriptures. "Everything is in the Book," she declares. "You've got to read His word if you want to get close to him. Joshua 1 and 8 is the scripture I always read."

She also counsels trust in the Lord for anyone wrestling with a severe personal problem.

"Don't give up your faith if you're struggling with something," she asserts. "I know it's so easy to say and hard to do, but don't give up. There has to be an inward fight.

"If you lose that fighting on the inside, you really will give up. Keep the fight going—just keep going. You've got to remember that all help comes from the Lord. If you remain humble, God will exalt you."

REV. MILTON BIGGHAM

Photo by David Booker

Milton wears more hats—or as many hats—as anyone does in the field of gospel music. It's a wonder that sometimes those hats aren't confusing to him.

Besides being a producer, a record label executive, and an artist himself, he is also a writer, musician, and preacher—he pastors his own church in New Jersey.

He's a great counselor and a very intelligent individual. I'm impressed with his general acumen about life. Milton has stretched a little bit beyond the other people in his field in that he continually strives to do bigger and better things.

His experience with Whitney Houston and writing the sound track for *The Preacher's Wife*, was a very wonderful highlight for many of us in the gospel music industry in that there was movie recognition of our music.

Milton places the industry in a position where the rest of the world can see that we not only have a good message, but that we manage what we do well, so that the message is carefully guided and put into the right places.

And that's the goal of this Lord's soldier.

$\mathcal{W}$hen the two-time Grammy Award–winning singer and producer arrived in Vietnam as a young infantryman, Milton had many troubling questions churning in his mind about God.

By the time the founder and lead singer of the acclaimed Georgia Mass Choir left that bloody battlefield, he not only had answers to many of his questions, but also a profound sense of gratitude for the miracles the Lord had sent his way to save his life.

"I walked in not really knowing how to pray, and I walked out with prayer on my lips," proclaims the Savoy Records star and pastor. "I walked in with just a minor relationship with God, and I walked out with an incredible relationship."

Calling to mind his childhood days growing up on a rural south Georgia farm, Milton recalls how Barwick, located about thirty miles from Tallahassee, Florida, was "a small country town where my grandparents had a little farm. My granddaddy was doing what you'd call share-cropping."

Milton, who lived with his grandparents on that farm until he was ten, doesn't remember doing much farmwork himself. Instead, he recalls being a quiet and studious youngster who mostly occupied himself with school and church. "In school I enjoyed writing. I liked the art of writing. I liked just using the pencil. I would get the writing book and just draw words—I loved that."

The local Baptist church was also a special treat for the talented youngster, especially when his grandfather, Deacon A. C. Smith, was leading the devotionals there. It was at this church that Milton first developed his love of gospel music.

"The unique thing about being raised there, is that I had a chance to watch my grandfather," he states. "I pay so much tribute to him. I even recorded a song and dedicated it to him, because he was such a great inspiration in my life as a young boy."

Milton portrays his grandfather not only as an incredibly hard worker who spent hours of backbreaking work in the fields, but also as someone who possessed such an incredible voice that he would literally hold his congregation spellbound with his vocal abilities.

"He impressed me so greatly. I mean, much of what I know today in terms of musical ability, and being able to stand and sing in front of people, I got it from looking at Granddaddy.

"He'd travel from church to church throughout south Georgia and sing. And he mesmerized me whenever I would go to church. But more than that, he would sing around the house whenever he was getting ready to go to church. I believe my musical ability was inherited through my grandfather—and my mother also got her talent from him."

Milton, who when he is not touring with his Grammy-, Stellar-, and Dove-nominated choir can be found preaching from the pulpit at the Mount Vernon Baptist Church in Newark, New Jersey, makes no secret of having been born out of wedlock.

"I think it's vital to talk about that," the singer, song-writer, and pastor asserts. "My mom was a young gospel singer who wound up having—if you want to call it that—an affair with my father. And, of course, I was the by-product.

"But she wanted to travel and sing. She was associated with Roberta Martin, and Brother Joe Mayse. These people at that time were very prominent gospel singers.

"She wanted to further her career, so she continued traveling and singing. And everybody in the family wanted her to be successful, so my grandfather and my grandmother didn't have any problem about me staying with them. And that's what I did until age ten, when my mom decided to come and get me."

Having been raised by two elderly relatives did not result in a lonely childhood, he contends. In fact, the faith-driven vocalist describes his childhood days as just the opposite.

"I had an uncle who was about the same age as me," he recalls. "And he and I grew up together and we had fun. There were always exciting things to do. Like I remember the first time I sang in church."

The singer and pastor laughingly recalls being about eight years old when he made his singing debut before an amused and appreciative church audience. "My uncle and I sang a duet in the Easter program, there in Barwick," he says with a chuckle. "I remember it was such an exciting thing to me.

"And I remember the next day, the Monday when we got to school, a lot of the young people and my teacher had heard about it. They complimented us. And I remember what a good feeling that was. It felt good—and it never has, from that day to this, felt bad."

Besides acquiring his love of music from his grandparents, the accomplished artist and record company producer also remembers how they always instructed him on religious matters.

"I always liked that. There was never a time when I felt uncomfortable listening to them tell me about the Lord," he recalls. "My grandmother, Leah, wasn't as much of a singer as my grandfather, but she was a regular churchgoer and a big influence in my religious training."

Milton's farm days came to an end when his mother, now married to a minister, returned to her parents' house to fetch her young son. She and Milton headed off to Texas so that he could meet his new stepfather.

"We were living in the parsonage of the church in Lamesa, Texas, because my stepfather was a preacher," he recollects. "So when I got to Texas I right away became involved with a church, and it was like a home-coming for me."

For the next several years the gospel star remembers doing a lot of traveling with his mother between Texas and Florida as she continued her gospel singing career. Along the way, the teenager was learning to become quite a performer himself.

"I remember it was in Texas that I sang with my mother for the first time. I was sixteen or thereabouts. That's when I started playing the piano—I took some lessons.

"Before that, there was an old upright piano at my grandparents' house that I used to tinker with. I loved traveling with her and being called on to do a song."

During those months when the family was back home in Texas, Milton continued to pursue his love of music. "I started playing for the choir at church, and I did some singing at school. I just kind of started learning how to find my way around the keyboards."

Milton recalls how difficult it often was to find gospel music on radio stations in the Lone Star State, where country music filled the airwaves. But on Sunday nights the teenager was able to tune in a gospel show that was being broadcast out of Nashville.

"That was my lifeline to gospel music," Milton recollects. "It was a ritual for me to listen to that station every Sunday night after church. I'd go to my room, and tune in WLAC, which sometimes I could hardly get.

"I would pray for a clear night so the station would come in. Then I would take that, what I heard, and go to church and try to duplicate it on the piano. And that's the way it was. I was very attracted to gospel music.

"Everything I could get my hands on, I'd listen to. Anytime a musician came to our church who could play well, I would always talk to him, and try to get a chord or something."

Milton and his family relocated again, this time to Winter Haven, Florida, where the teenager could often be found after high school singing or playing piano at one local church event or another.

Milton laughingly recalls that, "In Winter Haven I became virtually a star at high school. That's because in the eleventh grade we had talent shows, and I was the only kid in high school who could play all the latest popular stuff, as well as gospel.

"Then I started playing the organ for this church in Tampa, Florida. It was called The New Mount Zion Baptist Church, and it was a large church. I guess it was one of the largest black churches in Tampa at that time, and it still is now.

"And playing the organ there, it really gave me some exposure. That's when I started really seriously looking into gospel music in terms of being an original artist."

His dream to become a gospel artist would have to be put on hold because of something called the Vietnam War. At the time, Milton was attending the Miami Barber College, learning a skill that in the months to come would save his life.

Milton received his draft notice in 1966. "I was inducted into the armed forces, and I went immediately into the infantry. I started training for Vietnam."

Milton recalls that it was when he had completed his basic training that he experienced his first challenge to his faith. "You know, there had never been a time in my life when I questioned my faith," he states. "I never wanted to do anything else but gospel, and I'd always been in church. My faith never wavered as it relates to whether I wanted to stay within the church or get out of the church.

"Well, if there ever was a time when I lost my faith, this was it. It was a time when it got rough for me to keep it. I questioned God at that point about all that I had done musically for Him: Why would He choose me to go to Vietnam rather than some other guys?"

It was a question he wrestled with constantly throughout his long sea voyage to that Southeast Asia country. But no answer was forthcoming. "By the time I got to Vietnam I was convinced that this was *where* He wanted me to be, so I didn't question Him anymore. It wasn't until I came home that I realized *why* He had sent me there.

"It was to teach me who He is. And He did that! It was to teach me to rely totally on Him. And He showed me that I could trust Him. He taught me trust over there. And He also gave me faith—Vietnam gave me faith. And it taught me humbleness. Vietnam gave me the answers to my questions, but it took a year for Him to talk to me and to prove His power."

The answers that Milton sought came amidst some of the heaviest fighting of the war. As he recounts the events that led up to his understanding of why God sent him overseas, his voice takes on an almost reverent quality.

"You know, I don't talk too much about this," he professes. "I don't want people to think that I'm just spinning war stories. What I'm telling you I've only told a few people, because many people just wouldn't understand it. But it needs to be printed, because the world needs to know."

Milton takes a deep breath before beginning his stirring testimony of how three times God intervened to save his life.

"I remember that it was a tropical summer and I was up in this place near Khe San," he begins. "And one day we were walking from the brush to the school—it was a torn-up building that we knew the Vietnamese had used as a school.

"We were walking from the wood-line area to the school, which was in an open space. All of my company had gotten into the school, and me and this other guy were the last out in the clearing."

Just as he and his partner were approaching the middle of the clearing, shots rang out. "We realized that we were being ambushed, and there was a firefight that lasted about five to ten minutes."

What happened next is still kind of fuzzy. All Milton can recall of those ten minutes is that they seemed to go by like hours as he lay with his face buried in the ground, while bullets whizzed over his head.

He still remembers wondering whether one of those bullets was marked for him. "It was, you know, like you see it in the movies, when the dirt is flying up after bullets hit it. That's what I was seeing."

Lying there, Milton knew that if he and his partner didn't quickly get to cover, they weren't going to make it. "I said to the guy, 'We can't stay here. We gotta get outta here—we gotta move.' "

With bullets whizzing over their heads, the two men ran for their lives. "The firing was going on and he started running and I started running behind him, zigzagging. It was the longest run of my life.

"When we got into the school we jumped inside. He didn't know it, and I didn't know it either, but he was

shot. And I was right *behind* him"—Milton places emphasis on that word—"and I never got shot."

It was only later, when his heart had stopped pounding with fear and exertion, and the patrol had returned to
camp, that Milton says he realized he had just been
blessed with a life-saving miracle. All logic suggested that
he should have been the one to take a bullet in the back—
not the man in front of him! But all Milton suffered was
an injury to his leg, which would later factor into another
life-saving miracle.

"I didn't think about that when it happened," he submits. "I was trying to live, I was trying to stay alive. It was
only later that I realized that I was the one that should've
got shot."

There was a second time when God intervened to save
the young soldier's life. "What happened is that I was
staying out in the 'boon,' as we called it.

"I was out there for six months. And one day we
went on a patrol. And we came upon a Vietnamese
camp. We had a firefight and they ran off and left everything."

Milton remembers rummaging through stuff that the
enemy had left behind, when he discovered an ammuni-
tion can. "I opened the can and there was an old set of
clippers. This guy who had the can was a barber. There
were two hand clippers, and there were razor blades, and
there were shears."

Milton turned to a soldier standing nearby.

"Hey, this guy was a barber."

The soldier shrugged. "Well, so what?"

Milton smiled, shrugged, and threw the barber's kit
down to the ground.

"I was on my way out of the camp—everybody had
left the area. I was about two hundred yards away, and a
voice spoke to me and said: 'Go back and get the can.'
This voice spoke to me in my head.

"So I went back and got the can, took it back to base camp. Over the next two weeks I learned how to cut hair with those hand clippers, 'cause I'd been to barber college. I started cutting all the guys' hair around the camp."

One morning about three weeks later, Milton was suddenly summoned by his captain, a black officer, who asked the soldier to bring his barber kit with him.

"He said, 'I've been hearing about you cutting hair, and I want you to give me a haircut.' Well, I was very nervous, but I gave him his haircut. And after I cut his hair, he looked in the mirror.

"And he said, 'Man, I can't believe this. This is the best haircut I've ever had. And you're doing it with hand clippers. Okay, I want you to come every other week and cut my hair.' So that's what happened. Every other week I had to go cut his hair."

Milton recalls that a close friendship between him and his captain gradually developed. One day, the officer told Milton that he planned to transfer the barber to a base camp located in a secure location. Milton was flabbergasted. "He said, 'I'm gonna send you in.' I said: 'Thank you, sir.'"

A month passed, and Milton heard no further word about his transfer. Meanwhile, new orders had come through. "We finally got a call to go further north—and we went to the worst place that we'd ever been.

"I sat up on a hill for a week and literally watched guys die. And all this time I was waiting for my captain to say, 'Biggham, you can go in.' But he never said it."

Milton's patrol received its latest orders. They were told to prepare to face the enemy. "Now the word came down that we had to go down to this camp, where the Vietnamese regulars were. We had never fought them before. But we sat there all that week and saw our guys get killed, so we knew how tough they were.

"I was scared. Everybody was scared. I was sitting in my hooch—my tent—scared and praying. It was raining and I was as scared as I've ever been in my life.

"And all of a sudden, about eight o'clock that night, the same guy who came to get me to cut the captain's hair came to the door and said, 'Biggham, the captain says in the morning he's gonna send you in.' "

Milton could not believe what he was hearing. Just as he was about to face certain death, he had received a reprieve. This time there was no delay in his thinking that he had been blessed with a second, life-saving miracle.

"The next morning, as my company was going down the hill to this firefight, I was walking the opposite way, going to a helicopter. By the time I got from the helicopter into the base camp, I was hearing about guys getting killed. And here I was, spared, all because the Lord told me to go back and get those clippers."

There was one final time when the gospel music star believes that God performed a miracle to save his life. "I had one more month left in that country, and then I was coming home," he recalls. "Well, that captain I had befriended left, and we got a new captain.

"And he decided everybody who was in base camp had to go back to the field and fight again. So here I was—I hadn't fought in four or five months—and he sends for me."

Milton had convinced his captain friend just before his transfer to allow him to see a medic because of problems he was having with his leg. "If you could get something that was called a 'profile' on anything that was wrong with you, you didn't have to go back and fight," he explains.

"Your leg is terrible," the doctor said, when Milton appeared before him the following morning. Under ordinary circumstances, such news might have been distressing. But Milton smiled, feeling relieved.

"Well, if it's that bad, do I get out of going back into the infantry?" he asked the doctor.

The doctor shook his head sideways. "No."

Milton was shocked. "But, sir, you just said—"

"I'm not gonna give you a profile," the doctor coldly interrupted. "You gotta go and fight like everybody else."

Dejected, he remembers returning to his tent, only to hear a voice speaking to him that Milton recognized. It was the very same one that had urged him to pick up the barber's kit.

"So I knew this was God speaking to me. And He said, 'Don't worry about it.' The next morning I went over to my sergeant as though I had not seen a doctor at all.

"I told him I needed to go see another doctor. So there I was standing in line waiting to see the doctor. There was an American doctor and an Oriental doctor. And as your turn came up, you'd see whatever doctor was available."

Relying on some deep, intuitive sense, Milton remembers thinking that it was imperative that he be examined by the Chinese doctor. "I was convinced in my spirit that I had to go to the Oriental doctor.

"I just knew that he was the one I had to see. But there was a problem: I couldn't make that decision, because when it was your turn you saw the doctor that was free.

"So now I'm three guys away—there's two guys standing in front of me. If the guys moved as they were supposed to, I would get the Oriental doctor. Except, when the last guy gets ready to see the doctor, the Oriental doctor takes a break."

Milton pauses, laughter in his voice. "You might think I'm just making this up, but it's the truth. So while he's on his break, the guy in front of me went to see the American doctor.

"Well, I'm next in line and just before the American doctor finishes with this guy, the Oriental doctor comes back in. So I walked right over to him. Now mind you, I got a month left in the country and I need a profile."

The doctor looked at the young soldier.

"Mr. Biggham, what's your problem?"

"I have a knee problem."

"How long do you have left in the country?" the doctor asked, smiling.

"I've got thirty days."

"Let's do an X-ray."

When the doctor returned with the X-ray, he was shaking his head sympathetically.

"Your knee is terrible," he said, examining the X-ray.

"I know."

"I'm gonna give you a thirty-day profile."

Milton still remembers releasing the longest sigh of relief in his life. "He knew I only had that amount of time left. And he looked at me, and he smiled. And he said, 'If you have any trouble after that, come see me. I'll take care of you.'

"It was just incredible. I remember that day as if it were just yesterday. It looked like God had just taken the whole world and put everything together for me. And I really began to understand why I was in Vietnam.

"God was refining me. He was getting rid of impurities in me, negative thoughts, and showing me, when I questioned Him, that there was no need to question Him. He's in charge.

"Look what he had done for me in such chaos. And what he had just done for me with that doctor. So I stayed there for another thirty days and I walked out of Vietnam alive."

Today, reflecting back on that harrowing time of his life, the award-winning artist emotionally testifies: "I walked in with questions, and I walked out with answers. I walked in in darkness, and I walked out in a marvelous light. I walked in with a negative attitude, and I walked out with a positive attitude.

Upon returning home, Milton decided to do something that he had been thinking about for months. He studied to become a minister. "When I got back I wasn't prompted to go into the ministry, I just *knew* that I had to. I simply knew that God and I now had a relationship that could not be broken."

After settling back into civilian life, Milton recalls how eager he was to resume his gospel music pursuits. "I got back and I was gung ho. Not only did I conquer Vietnam, but I had conquered myself in the process—and my beliefs. I was now just ready to do whatever I needed to do."

In Florida, he put his plan into action. "I wanted to do something unique with my career," he declares. "I wanted to put something together. So I put a group together called the Gospel Faith Increases—my first group. We basically sang stuff that everybody else had sung."

But Milton remembers not being satisfied with the result of his effort. So he went on to form another choir: the fifteen-member New Redemptive Ensemble. He then convinced a local record studio owner to let him record a demo of his new choir.

"I didn't have any money, but I said to him, 'Just let me record and let me bring my group out.' And he could hear what we do, and he could take the music and sell it, and do whatever he wanted to do with it. I just wanted the opportunity to record."

The studio owner agreed. With the demo in hand, Milton attended the Gospel Music Workshop of America in New Orleans, where he eventually got the demonstration record into the hands of a talent scout for Savoy Records.

When months passed and nothing came of that contact, Milton became convinced that the demo had been tossed into the nearest wastebasket. He was wrong.

"Meanwhile, I went on to form a gospel group called the Tampa Mass Choir, and it became pretty important around the area. Then one day, out of the blue, I got a call from a guy named John Daniels, who worked at Savoy Records."

Milton still remembers how surprised he was to hear from the record company after so many months. "They knew about the New Redemptive Ensemble—they had heard that demo—and they knew about me.

"They were looking to record a lady in Florida, and they wanted a choir to back her up. They asked if I would consider working with this lady and doing a recording."

It was the opportunity of a lifetime and Milton eagerly accepted. "I wrote about ninety percent of the songs on that record and Savoy put it out. I now had a relationship with that record company."

That relationship intensified when, in 1976, Milton decided to move to New York City. First on his agenda was a visit to his record company. Milton recalls that the last thing he expected after that visit was to be offered a job as the company's director of promotions.

Milton held that position for two years before being promoted to a producer, where his accomplishments over the years were second to none. He went on to win two Grammy Awards, the most recent as producer of the Best Soul Gospel Performance, *Live at Carnegie Hall* by the late Rev. James Cleveland.

He also produced such popular gospel stars as LaShun Place, Albertina Walker, and the Rev. Timothy Wright. Milton's duties as a producer, however, did not distract him from his own creative efforts.

"I was still writing and doing my songs," he offers. "I was recording and performing with some of the biggest names in gospel music, such as Albertina Walker, the Mississippi Mass choir, Dorothy Norwood, Inez Andrews, and James Cleveland."

Today, the artist, writer, producer, and pastor is, perhaps, best known for his lead singer duties with one of the most acclaimed choirs in gospel music—the Georgia Mass Choir.

Milton attests that one of the reasons why he founded the choir was to honor the state where he spent so many happy days as a youngster.

"I just wanted to do something for Georgia. I was remembering my granddaddy, and I wanted to do something for home," he declares. "I thought, why not do a mass choir?

"So I called some friends of mine and I told them my idea and they went for it. The first rehearsal we had in Macon, Georgia—I'll never forget it—six hundred people showed up. The Georgia Mass was birthed out of that; that was thirteen years ago."

Although Milton's grandfather is no longer alive to appreciate the musical legacy he passed on to the little boy who used to watch him sing in church, the gospel music star's mother still lives in Florida.

"She loves every minute of what I'm doing. She's even more gung ho than I am," he declares. "She's a singer from the heart." Milton discloses that he has a big surprise in store for his mother. "I want her to sing with the choir. I'm thinking about doing that on the next Georgia Mass recording session."

Despite all his success—including writing six of the songs that he and his choir performed in the hit movie *The Preacher's Wife*—Milton admits there are still days when problems get him down.

It is at such moments, the accomplished entertainer discloses that he lifts his spirits by thinking about the miracles he experienced while serving in Vietnam.

"Whenever something comes up that I think I can't handle, I'm reminded of what He did for me in Vietnam," he assents. "And I know that if I overcame that—if He took me through that—He can take me through this. And it never fails. 'Cause the experiences I've had on this side cannot compare to what I went through in Vietnam."

Milton, who has led his choir in performances before worldwide audiences from Israel to the Philippines, recollects one particular evening when his gratitude to the Lord spilled over into tears.

"I was in Italy one night—I was there with Reverend Clay Evans—and we were getting ready to go onstage. I remember that I was sitting in the dressing room with an older evangelist who was there with us. And that night, just when we were ready to go on, I couldn't help it. I was just sitting there, and tears started coming. And it was just uncontrollable. I just tried to get hold of myself, and I couldn't do it. I mean, I was just crying, crying, crying, and I *had* to talk to somebody."

Milton turned to the evangelist for comfort. "I said, 'Here I am, in Italy, about to go onstage and perform for hundreds of people, and I'm remembering the day that I was in that ambush.' It's just unbelievable that God has brought me from that to this. I can't believe that God is so awesome."

When Milton was finished, the evangelist softly replied: "Let me tell you what God is trying to tell you," she said. "He's trying to tell you that you owe Him. You owe Him a thank you, and He's reminding you of that. Cry. Get it out. But enjoy. All He wants you to do is to remember.' "

Milton says he does a lot of remembering, whether it's from his pulpit at the Mount Vernon Baptist Church, or at the many gospel music workshops he conducts throughout the United States.

What he always tries to impart to his audiences is that they, too, can experience God's blessings if they simply keep Him in mind. "Don't focus on your problems, don't focus on other people—your first focus should be on God," he advises. "Put yourself in His hands and just let God do what He wants to do.

"He doesn't always speak to you through burning bushes, or by causing fire to fall from heaven, or in the middle of a war. He knows how to speak to you through your mentality, through everyday things. And you've just got to learn how to listen. And there's something else you've got to learn, and it may sound like a cliché—but you've got to just let God."

EDWIN HAWKINS

Photo courtesy of PAZ Entertainment

Edwin is the father of contemporary gospel music. Because of his presentation of "Oh Happy Day," gospel was able to break into previously unknown markets—and thank God for that.

His vocal agility is fine as well, and his continued creativity in his workshops and seminars brings about a newness and a freshness in the gospel music industry. He continuously strives to do that.

Edwin is so debonair, and has such an unusual technique of working with people, that anybody would fall in love with him because of the love that he gives back. He'll always have a special place in the history of gospel music, and that can't be denied.

He is responsible for the familiarity of the Hawkins Family. That Walter, and Tramaine, and his sister, Lynette, have been able to have a musical platform is because he introduced them first through his "Oh Happy Day" presentation.

He is a Pentecostal and has had a Pentecostal experience all of his life, as is evidenced by his testimony. Edwin is not at all derelict in being able to communicate what the Lord has done for him in many situations—and continues to do!

Edwin Hawkins certainly has been touched by God.

*S*ince the day that he played piano on the legendary Hawkins Family's debut album at age seven, the "God-father of Gospel Music" had always dreamed about becoming a gospel artist.

What the multi-Grammy award winner did not realize, however, was the harsh price he would have to pay for accomplishing his dream—one that plunged him into a prolonged state of depression.

The Sony Music star entered that nightmarish twilight zone at age twenty-four, after successfully recording "Oh Happy Day," considered the greatest gospel hit of all time.

Instead of praise from the gospel community, Edwin was condemned and ridiculed by many Christians for secularizing praise music.

It was in the midst of this ordeal that the California native believes he was touched by God. And the words he heard during that moment convinced him that he was not a sinner but, instead, was doing the Lord's work. The four-time Grammy winner has never looked back since.

Today, instead of bitterness, Edwin is grateful for the lessons he learned during that ordeal. "For years and years and years I would say, 'God, why, why, why? I mean, why me?' And then one day I said: 'Why not me?' What it made me learn is that I'm no better than anybody else, you know?

"God allows those thorns to be there. Sometimes we let those thorns get the best of us—the best of our flesh and the best of our faith. We get tricked and fooled by the enemy and we focus on those thorns. What we don't understand is that God allowed those thorns to temper us and to humble us and then use us for His good."

Born one of the middle of eight children, Edwin was reared in the housing projects of the tough Campbell Village section of Oakland, California. Most of what he learned about religion came from his mother, whom he describes as a "devout Christian," while his father was not.

"My dad was a longshoreman, and he came to know Christ later on in his life, in the early seventies, when my brother, Walter, was called to the ministry and started his own church," Edwin explains.

Both parents, however, always impressed upon the youngster the importance of loving and respecting other people.

"We were brought up in the Church of God in Christ, and my spiritual lessons at home had a lot of 'do unto others as you'd have them do to you,' " he relates. "I was taught not to tell lies, to try to love everybody, and treat everybody the same."

Edwin still vividly recalls how his mother put into practice what she preached. "We actually saw her live that life," he declares. "We often saw her taking in some other child that wasn't doing well with his parents, or whose parents didn't treat him right. As a small kid I always remember my mother really trying to help somebody out."

It was an example that, years later, the acclaimed gospel star would follow when he established the popular Edwin Hawkins Music and Arts Seminar, a showcase for future gospel artists and a way for them to hone their skills under Edwin's tutelage.

"In my travels, I ran into many talented young folks whose only outlet to sing gospel music was found in the church," he explains. "There needed to be a way to help them further develop their skills and abilities to the glory of God.

"So I decided to help them find themselves in the arts. I felt it incumbent upon me to marshal the finest artists and musicians to teach these youngsters."

Since the 1980s, when Edwin first began the program, more than five thousand youngsters have gathered each summer at the seminar's Florida location. Over the years, the annual music convention, which offers classes on everything from songwriting to choir decorum, has been the springboard for many of today's top gospel artists.

The value of encouragement is something that Edwin understands very well, because his own musical career was built upon it. He grew up in a family that played and sang music, and Edwin remembers how his parents, Mamie and Dan Lee, always supported his musical pursuits.

When he was seven years old, Edwin was not only already singing in youth choirs, but was such a good piano player that he took over full-time piano playing duties for the Hawkins family group, which released its first recording in 1957.

"Music ran in my family," he humbly submits. "My mother and most of her brothers were musical. She was one of eleven children and one of her brothers was even a jazz musician.

"So we heard some of that in our home. My mother didn't close any music out just because she was a Christian. She wasn't like some Christians we knew who wouldn't allow jazz to be listened to at home.

"We listened to it all, and we were always singing, whether it was in the church choir or as a family group.

Before I came along my mother used to play the piano for us. Then I came along and started playing for the family."

Edwin laughingly recalls that, as a child, he was so enthralled by music that he often spent more time at the piano than watching television. "There was always a piano in the house," he recollects. "I'm not even sure where that piano came from. I just know I was always being encouraged to play it since I was five—maybe even before that."

But despite his obvious talent, the gospel music star recollects he was rather timid about performing in public.

"I was an introverted and very, very shy person," he discloses. "But because I was talented I always sang when I played the piano. A lot of people who watched me play the piano misunderstood me and thought that I was a very aggressive kid. They just didn't know how shy I really was."

Besides his musical activities at home, Edwin demonstrated his piano playing and singing talents both in school and church. "We used to go to the Good Samaritan Church of God in Christ. It was in Oakland," he recalls. "I enjoyed it. It was a big part of my life."

At church, the youngster so impressed the congregation with his musical abilities, that word quickly spread about the remarkably talented boy.

Edwin soon found himself performing at several local churches in the area, as well as on a weekly Sunday night radio broadcast, all before he was sixteen years old! "It was God who just pushed me out onstage and told me to do it," he offers. "I was pushed to perform by my parents, my friends, and even the Lord."

The accomplished entertainer, whose phenomenal musical career spans nearly fifty years on the big stages of the world, believes he was twice "touched by the Lord": once at age sixteen, and, later, when the joy of having a hit record turned into a nightmare.

Edwin first recalls God's strong presence in his life when, as a teenager, he decided to make a serious commitment to Jesus. "I had left my former church and joined the Ephesian Church of God in Christ, which was pastored by Tramaine's [Hawkins] grandfather," he relates.

"I remember that there often were revivals at that particular church and I was at one of them. And during the service there'd always be an altar appeal for those who wanted to give their hearts to the Lord."

There was one particular Sunday morning when the teenager decided he wanted to be one of those who went up to the altar to give his heart to Jesus. He recalls the moment as one when "a very spiritual awakening was taking place in me—I was feeling the presence of God. And I also remember walking up to that altar.

"I was just sixteen, but I felt responsible enough to know that I needed to make a serious commitment as a Christian. Although we were raised in the ghetto, I was never really a street kid. I spent most of my time in church."

As a result, the youngster reasoned that if he was going to continue spending as much time as he already was in church, it was only right that he make "that kind of serious commitment—to try to understand what Christianity was all about.

"I didn't want to say that I was a Christian because my mother was. I can still remember thinking about my mother's life, the way she practiced her Christianity. And what I saw her do in her life really influenced me to want to be a Christian."

When the moment came for him to give his life to the Lord, the acclaimed gospel star recalls that "it was like the Spirit of the Holy Ghost was taking over my body. The Church of God in Christ is a very emotional church—and I'm not an extremely emotional person, even today. But I do remember that what I went through was quite an emotional experience."

Edwin left the church that day feeling that "something had taken place in my life. I had made a serious commitment to the Lord as a Christian. And with time—it wasn't an overnight thing—I started to learn all about what it meant to be a Christian."

In 1967 Edwin took an important step toward launching his successful musical career. With the help of a singer named Betty Watson, the young entertainer organized the Northern California State Youth Choir.

A year later, he and Watson along with the choir recorded *Let Us Go into the House of the Lord.* When this album was released, critics noticed that there was something distinctly different about its gospel sound.

Although the album featured a traditional-sounding choir and vocalists, it had more of an R&B sound to it than anything previously recorded in gospel music.

On the album was one particular song, "Oh Happy Day," which attracted more than the usual attention from broadcasters and retailers alike. The cut, which was helped by a national promotional campaign, unusual for gospel music in those days, quickly crossed from gospel to the R&B charts.

It gained even more public appeal when an underground FM station in San Francisco began playing the cut. This led to "Oh Happy Day" eventually finding its way to the pop charts.

By the time the dust had settled, the record would sell an incredible seven million copies, win Edwin a Grammy Award in 1970, and start a new trend in gospel music— pioneering what is today called contemporary gospel.

"It was unforeseeable, but the reaction was explosive," he recalls. "It was a special thing that God had done for me."

At first Edwin was ecstatic over his success. The young gospel star was especially pleased that he was able to introduce spiritual music to a worldwide audience that had little or no exposure to it.

But what happened next was so discouraging that Edwin recalls giving serious thought to leaving the music business altogether. The young gospel star suddenly found himself under assault from members of the gospel community.

"We started to get a lot of ridicule, mainly from the church community," he recollects in a voice that still bears a trace of anger. "And it made me, you know, wonder and ask myself, 'Well, what is this all about?' We even had some ministers and pastors trying to get a petition to get the song off the secular radio stations, and that kind of confused me a bit."

Particularly upsetting was that the criticism did not mesh with what he had been brought up to believe about religion.

"It made me really begin to search the Word of God again," Edwin submits. "Because from when I was a child I was taught that the gospel should be spread to the 'highways and hedges,' that we should 'go into all the world.' Well, isn't the radio—secular radio—part of the world?"

As the onslaught continued, Edwin plunged into a deep state of depression.

"I was very disillusioned," he recollects. "I thought it was a great opportunity to share the gospel through song, and we were being criticized for it. The members of the chorus felt the same way. We were all living in Oakland at the time and we had a pretty large group."

Edwin recalls that one way he and members of his choir would deal with the attacks was to hold daily devotionals while on tour.

"We chose twelve o'clock to come together for devotion and Scripture reading and discussion," he recollects. "We had a lot of conversation about what was going on.

"We all felt together in this ridicule situation, and we discussed it among ourselves. And we prayed, and we meditated. We would ask each other, if this wasn't what God wanted us to do, why would He present the opportunity if it was so wrong? We felt that this was what God wanted."

Although there often were more questions than answers, the acclaimed gospel artist recalls that his faith in the Lord never wavered. What he does remember losing faith in was the various Christian denominations.

"You know, throughout that whole episode I never lost faith in God . . . and I didn't even lose faith in people. But it was denominations that I lost faith in. In all my Bible studies, I never once found that word. I found it in school, and that's where I learned about denominations and that what it means is to divide. God's body is not divided. Denominations come from man, not from God."

What Edwin mostly objected to was the conviction among some denominations that they were a kind of exclusive religious club. "I think we should be spreading the gospel to everyone the best we know. We should share the gospel and live the life, not just preach it and try to keep it exclusive. I was always taught to share the gospel—through song or whatever—with different groups of people, even though they might not believe the same that we believe.

"But now I learned that many Christians felt that just because someone was not within their denomination, or within their circle, they were not worthy of hearing the gospel message—and that's wrong. That's small-minded. When they start putting their righteousness in, that makes me mad. That kind of righteousness is not right before God."

Edwin recalls one particular evening when he was so bitterly attacked that he almost completely lost it. As the Lord would have it, it was just at that moment that he gained something in return: a message of encouragement from the Almighty.

"I can still clearly remember that we were performing at a club for professional managers in Hollywood," he testifies, "and we were playing there every night for two weeks.

"And I remember that one of the bishops—I don't even remember who he was, I don't think I had ever met him before—called me. He somehow knew which hotel I was staying in. And he rebuked me long-distance on the telephone."

When the harangue ended, the accomplished singer felt that things could not get much worse. "I hung up, and that's when I really began to cry and ask God about it. I fell on my knees."

Edwin relates with a note of awe in his voice how, during that moment of prayer, a gentle voice spoke to him, one that encouraged the young artist to read a Scripture concerning the Apostle Paul.

"I can't quote it to you, but it was about one planting the seed, and another coming along to water the seed—so that God can give the increase."

Edwin turned to the Scripture. He recalls that when he finally put the Holy Book down, the depression he was feeling suddenly began to lift. "It was a revelation for me," he recollects.

"Because whenever we would come back from a tour, we'd be asked with a condescending kind of attitude, 'Well, how many souls were saved?' and 'How many did you witness to?'—that kind of thing.

"And God showed me right there that it wasn't for me, necessarily, to know who or how many were saved for sure, because we don't know who is saved for sure, except through the spirit of God.

"But it was sometimes my job just to plant the seed—or maybe just water it—and then God would be the one to give the increase. And it was from that point that I realized that He called upon me to help Him do His job. That I was planting seeds for Him."

Now feeling rejuvenated for the first time in months, Edwin began to pick up the pieces of his life with some enthusiasm. The gifted singer and songwriter soon found himself performing at some of the world's biggest concert halls and reaching out to world audiences with his music and spiritual message.

He also became a mainstay on network television and countless radio programs. In addition, Edwin captured a variety of awards. He was nominated for ten Grammys and won four of them, the last one in 1983 for the song "If You Love Me."

"All these doors started opening for me after that evening," he recalls. "I guess you always emerge stronger from such spiritual tests."

Reflecting back on that time in his life, Edwin thinks he understands why it was necessary for him to undergo such an ordeal. He again uses Paul as a way to illustrate his point. "You know all the things that he did to Christians before he became a Christian. He killed them and rebuked them, and had them beaten and sent to prison. The Bible said that God allowed a thorn to be in his flesh.

"But that thorn was there to make him what God wanted him to be to shape him into the image of God and to humble him. I personally experienced that thorn. There was a reason for it and I didn't lose faith. It kept me from feeling too important about myself."

The musician, entertainer, and songwriter contends that some of today's gospel stars could also benefit from having a thorn in their side.

"So many of our gospel artists have been fooled and tricked by the enemy," he submits. "Sometimes they let the thorns get the best of their flesh or their faith.

"So often when I hear people brag about, you know, what they did on the road, or how successful it was, that's usually to their own glory. It's not giving glory to God.

"Some are sincere about the ministry of gospel music and some are not. For some it's just an easy situation where they can feel important and become a star. They need to feel the thorn the way I did to humble them."

From his own experience, Edwin offers that he is a firm believer in the positive effects of prayer. He adds that he does much of it in his private life.

"There's one thing I pray about all the time," he states. "It's the hope that as artists we can one day come together and understand that our physical or emotional struggles are there just to temper us, to make us what God wants us to be. It's not to fool us, not to trick us, not to make us fall. It's to humble us and shape us into the image of God."

Although Edwin believes he survived a major test of faith in the months following the release of "Oh Happy Day," he adds that there have been other challenges as well. One such challenge, he explains, has been to resist the temptation to perform secular music.

"Yeah, I've been tested again and again," Edwin proclaims. "It's always tempting to do other kinds of music than gospel. And, of course, record companies are always offering those kinds of opportunities to you. And I was offered them. I like all kinds of music. I can listen to any kind of music. In fact, when I've gone out to a supper club where they know I'm there, they may ask me to come to the mike and sing something. That's happened a few times.

"And I've done it and it's fun. But that's not what I do in terms of my ministry, so it was pretty easy for me to say to these record companies that's not the kind of music I want to do."

He adds with a laugh, "I may not always have done the right thing, but my heart has always been in the right place." Although the accomplished singer makes a joke of it, behind the lighthearted remark is a deadly serious point that he is trying to make.

"I know there are a lot of people who feel that they're not good enough to be Christians, that they might at some time have not done the right thing," he explains. "But I think the special thing about God is that it doesn't matter what your background is or what you've done.

"It doesn't matter where you've come from and who you think you are, how bad you are, or how good you think you are. We're all the same to God. He loves us all the same. What's most important is that you acknowledge that He is God. And that Jesus is the son of God, and that he came and died for our sins."

For anyone seeking to know God better, Edwin emphasizes that it is essential to devote time to Him. "If you say that you're a believer, it's important that you live what you say you believe," he counsels. "You have to understand that the relationship you have with Jesus Christ is just as important—if not more so—than it is with the person you say you love.

"When you love someone, then you spend time getting to know that person. So it's important that as Christians we spend committed time with Jesus Christ—in the Word, studying the Word, praying, communicating with Him."

Nowadays, Edwin is doing less live performing than in past years. Instead, the acclaimed entertainer is more focused on his songwriting, producing, and promotion of upcoming talent. One of his many recent projects was a new radio version of "Oh Happy Day."

He also hopes to continue to serve as something of a gadfly to the gospel industry, which the accomplished entertainer is sometimes critical of.

"You know, some of us have been called just to do music. Some of us have been called to preach and do music," he asserts. "But we all have to understand what the gospel is all about—and not all of these artists and record companies do.

"I don't need to name them. They know who they are. I just wish they would stop doing that. We can have a good time and have fun, but we also need to take gospel a little bit more seriously if we're going to use the word *gospel.* It implies a ministry. It is what Jesus told every believer to do: to share the gospel with the world."

That responsibility is something that Edwin feels some in the gospel industry fail to live up to. "You know, at the risk of sounding too judgmental, I look forward to the day when the industry as well as our gospel artists truly understand that definition.

"I guess what I'm trying to say is that while it's okay to become commercial—because I think we have to do that so that the world can hear the gospel in whatever form we can present it—all of our gospel people have to clearly understand their role in the ministry.

"You know, what we have to give as an industry is the best we know how to do. We have a great responsibility. I pray about that, too. The artists, the preachers—anyone that's visible before the public—has to show that although there're lots of things that are wrong in the world, we still live by the Word."

YOLANDA ADAMS

Photo by Peter Nash, Nashville, TN

Yolanda is my tall, wonderful, gorgeous friend. I have watched her grow from being a choir singer to being a superstar within the gospel music realm.

She also stands very tall in her ability to communicate her messages to her audiences, and she does have cross-over appeal, which I think is very good for us in this industry as well.

With her exposure on several network television shows, such as *The Tonight Show* with Jay Leno and others of that nature, she has exposed gospel music even more.

Her international appeal is great as well. She's traveled to Europe many times to give performances there. Yolanda's wardrobe, by the way, is always impeccable, as is her ability to host gospel music shows.

So Yolanda Adams is a true gospel star and one to be reckoned with as a soldier and a Kingdom builder.

*Y*olanda was only thirteen years old when her father died, and the heavy responsibility for bringing her family through this crisis fell upon her young shoulders.

It was a responsibility, the four-time Grammy nominee recalls, that she was not certain she had the strength to bear.

So Yolanda turned to the only person she could think of to ask for the strength to guide her family: the Lord.

And her prayers were quickly answered.

"He built my faith and He gave me the strength to take care of my mother, my brothers, and sisters while we were going through all this," declares the thirty-three-year-old Stellar and Dove award winner. "He gave me the extra strength that I needed when I needed it."

Out of gratitude, the Tribute Records sensation, who is currently studying to become a licensed minister, today communicates her love for God using a voice infused with a unique blend of jazz, gospel, and R&B.

It is through these lyrical declarations of her devotion to the Lord that the stylish six-foot-one-inch former Houston elementary school teacher, who once considered a career in modeling, encourages others in their own faith.

"He took me from where I was to where I am today, and I'll never forget that," declares the statuesque beauty, who is frequently compared to Whitney Houston and Anita Baker. "When you're facing obstacles, that's when you need to turn and face Him."

Yolanda credits her parents for her faith in the Lord. She contends it was through their efforts that she has always had a solid biblical foundation, and that those lessons continue to keep her spiritually grounded and down to earth while in the celebrity spotlight.

The eldest of six siblings, the versatile vocalist describes the Houston neighborhood where she was reared as being "like a big family. It was a black community with a few white families—and we played with them, too," she recollects. "People from other streets would come over and play on our streets, and ours was the busiest street. It was just a very nice neighborhood."

The stunning beauty doesn't remember herself as being a particularly good-looking youngster. Instead, she has memories of being an awkward and gangly girl who was rather shy and on the studious side. "I read everything. I was not wild and outgoing; I was the kind of kid that always tested the waters first," she laughingly admits.

Music was as important to her family life as religion, she recollects. "My father was a junior high school coach and a teacher, and my mom was also a teacher, on the elementary school level," Yolanda relates. "And they were both involved with the church. My dad was a good singer; he sang in the church choir.

"And my mom, she played the piano at her church. So church was a way of life for us. It wasn't just, Okay, we go to church on Sunday and that's it. Uh-uh. It really was a way of life for us."

The intelligent and quick-witted entertainer submits that she was literally born listening to gospel music. "Like I said, my mom used to play the piano at church. And I was almost born on the piano bench," Yolanda laughingly relates. "She was pregnant with me, and one week when she finished playing in the church she went straight to the hospital to have me."

Although her early musical influences weren't all from Christian traditions, Yolanda emphasizes that spiritual music always held a special place in her heart. "A lot of people don't think I should say this, but my influences in the music industry are people like Stevie Wonder and Nancy Wilson.

"My mom's degree was in music. So at home we listened to everything from classical to jazz to R&B and rock—everything.

"But gospel music was the heart of me. I was singing in the kids' choir at church when I was four. And, later, I was inspired by gospel artists like the Clark Sisters and O'Landa Draper."

When she wasn't singing, Yolanda could usually be found at home studying the Bible. "I was a pretty religious youngster," she recollects. "I'd come home from school, do my homework, and then it was nothing for me to go through the Psalms and find a nice one that I meditated on that day."

It's a practice that Yolanda says she engages in even today. "Ever since I was a kid I've taken the time to read the Word of God. I try to understand it. I try to get some meaning out of it. I think that's one of the reasons why I have a special relationship with God—because a lot of people don't take the time to do this."

The knowledge that she and the Lord had such a special relationship came to her when she was thirteen, the talented vocalist relates. "I was a young kid and this wasn't like a big 'wow' moment. It was just a realization.

"A lot of people have this great revelation, or this great tragedy, or this great whatever. But it didn't happen for me that way. And I thank God that it didn't happen for me that way.

"Because, for me, to understand that whatever the Lord wanted me to do was okay, expressed more of a love for Him than being pushed into what God wanted me to do."

Besides being taught to love and fear God, Yolanda remembers being taught by her parents to "love and respect other people. You know, we were brought up to love everybody," she says.

"We were brought up to know that everyone is special in God's sight, that we weren't the only ones. We learned that everyone has a place in God, and that God has something special for all of us to do. So we never held our nose up at anyone else."

As she grew into an attractive teenager, Yolanda submits that she cannot remember any single time when she rejected her spiritual lessons. "I can't think of any rebellious moments, especially not in my family," she asserts. "No drugs, no drinking—none of that stuff."

Instead, she developed leadership qualities, something that Yolanda credits her grandfather for instilling in her. "My grandfather told me a long time ago: 'You're gonna be the one that has to do all of this stuff because you're the oldest one. And if you don't, the other ones will have an excuse: Well, Yolanda didn't do it. . . .' "

That responsibility is something Yolanda not only took seriously as a young girl, but still does today in her role as a gospel music superstar. When she is not performing or attending classes at divinity school, Yolanda serves as the official spokesperson for Operation Rebound. That project takes her into inner-city schools where she talks to students about the perils of drugs and violence.

For the gifted songstress, life seemed almost magical until her world was suddenly shattered at age thirteen by the untimely death of her father. It was a sorrowful period for the young girl, who found herself responsible for keeping the family together.

"I guess it was my first test of faith," she asserts. "It wasn't like I said, 'God, I don't believe in you. God, are you really there?' It was more like, 'God, now you have to strengthen me, because it's really time for me to step up and be the oldest.'

"I was thirteen years old, and everybody under me was ten, nine, four, and three years old. And I had to be strong for my mother. Because she was really, really upset. You know, she was a young woman. She lost her husband at a very young age.

"My mom was thirty-two years old and my dad was thirty-five. So you know, for me to look at that today—for me to lose my husband, and we've only been married six-and-a-half months—can you imagine losing someone you were married to for thirteen years? It was devastating for her."

In the days following her father's death, the deeply saddened teenager turned to prayer and meditation for the strength to help her family carry on.

"Everyone's faith is tested all the time, and this was my time," she exclaims. "And my prayer to God was, 'Okay, God, I know this is a test. I know that this is something that I'm gonna have to deal with, because Dad's not coming back.'

"There was no bitterness toward God. There was sadness and there were definitely tears, because my dad and I were buddies. There was a sadness—but it was a good sadness—because I knew my dad was going to heaven."

Yolanda explains she was confident of that because her father had led such an exemplary life.

"You know, I was taught that when you give your life to God, and the purpose in your heart is to do what's right for God—and if you live a life as an example of what God would be if He were on earth—then you know that when He takes you you're going to a better place.

"And that was my satisfaction, so to speak. Yes, I was going to miss him—and I didn't know why he was no longer here. But I was not gonna question God. I knew that He had a reason for this, even though it hurt right now. Yeah, you do have those moments of 'This hurts.' But God understands that."

In the midst of her loss, the recording star remembers something very special that happened to her. "God did touch me. He gave me strength. It was miraculous!" she proclaims.

"I was strong for my mother and my siblings. God gave me the extra strength to pick the casket, pick the flowers, all that kind of stuff, because my mother was too emotional and too emotionally drained at that point. He built my faith and He gave me the strength to take care of my brothers and sisters while we were going through all this."

As she entered high school, the now stunning teenager with a six-foot-one-inch frame remembers giving serious consideration to becoming a fashion model. It was her grandfather who convinced Yolanda to do otherwise.

"Trust me, it was because of my grandfather," she says, laughing. "I had no reservations, nothing. I just *knew* I was gonna do that. And then my grandfather said: 'Now, remember, you're the oldest. Remember the conversation we had.

"'I'll tell you what. You go to college—you finish college—and as soon as you finish college I'll send you to New York, and I'll send you to Paris—I'll send you to wherever you want to go.

"'But you have to finish college, 'cause if you don't, the other ones won't. They'll use that as an excuse.' So, you know, being the oldest, you get the flack sometimes."

Again, Yolanda took her grandfather's advice, completing college with a degree in education. She then accepted a job teaching elementary school in Houston, Texas.

She did not, however, stop pursuing her love of music. During the summer months, Yolanda toured with the Southeast Inspirational Choir, and eventually became the choir's lead singer. "My daddy always told me to follow my dreams, and singing professionally was one of my dreams," she submits. "Singing meant the world to me."

Although the talented musician still had an affection for other types of music—from jazz to R&B—it was the emotional sincerity of gospel music that attracted her.

"It stemmed from my relationship with God," she declares. "I'm sure that other people can do the love songs, and make beautiful music, and still have their relationship with God. But as far as my upbringing and *my* conviction, I couldn't do it."

While singing with the Southeast Inspirational Choir, Yolanda came to the attention of the late prolific composer and producer Thomas Whitfield. Whitfield's confidence in the tall, skinny girl with the big voice led him to become her mentor and develop Yolanda's hit 1987 debut album, *Just As I Am.*

Quickly gaining national attention, Yolanda went on to sign with the Tribute Records label in 1990, and was hailed by one critic as the "best, most versatile, contemporary gospel vocalist since Aretha Franklin."

Moving effortlessly and comfortably between gospel, pop, jazz, soul, funk, and hip-hop, Yolanda went on to record three chart-topping hits on that label, earning numerous awards along the way.

Whatever kind of sound she was utilizing in her music, whether gospel or hip-hop, Yolanda emphasizes that the lyrics were always spiritual ones.

"Every type of music can be used as a ministry," she explains. "Ministry is influencing someone else to believe what you believe. We just tend to think that ministry is only for the church.

"I believe that God's message can be spread in a lot of different ways, and that's what I do. If television is the way, God bless the television set. I want to go into different avenues, like television and acting, and I want to be able to teach God's word through that."

In 1990 Yolanda experienced another challenge to her faith. Now in her midtwenties, the young gospel star was feeling discouraged over the slow pace of her career.

"I didn't have a record company, and I knew I was supposed to be singing," she relates. "I knew that I was born to do something like this, and it was like: 'Okay, when are we gonna do it?'"

So the gifted songstress sat down to have a little conversation with God.

"I told the Lord at that moment that I was disappointed. I prayed and asked the Lord, I said, 'Now, Lord, I *know* that this is what I'm supposed to do, because you told me this is what I'm supposed to do.

"'Why is it so difficult for these people to treat me right?' The record company I used to be with wasn't even responding to my calls, or sending me my checks. And I prayed for a few days, and I asked God for His guidance.

"I was getting my stuff out with God. You know, sometimes God will allow you to get your stuff out. He'll allow you to get the anger out. He'll allow you to get the feeling-sorry-for-yourself out.

"He'll allow you to have all of those emotions. And then, a few days later, He'll talk to you and say: 'Well, now that you've gotten all yours out, let me get mine out.'"

While in the midst of a silent prayer, Yolanda recalls hearing a voice speak to her, one with a mildly scolding tone to it. "It was the Lord speaking to me—I was certain of that.

"He said, 'Slow down, Yolanda. Be still. Know that I am still the same God that took care of you yesterday, and all the years before. I did tell you that this is what you're supposed to do, and because I told you, that should give you enough reason to trust me.' "

Falling down upon her knees, Yolanda remembers promising her Maker that never again would she entertain any doubts about Him. It is a promise the acclaimed singer has kept to this very day.

Since that time, Yolanda has proceeded to make four chart-topping, multi-award-winning albums, all of which have received Stellar Awards, the most prestigious prize offered by the gospel music industry.

To show her gratitude, the gifted songstress uses her broadly ranged voice to give tribute to the Lord, and enrolled in Howard University's highly accredited divinity program, preparing to become a licensed minister.

For anyone seeking to capture God's ear, Yolanda's best advice is to "sit down and understand the principles of prayer and meditation." In prayer, she goes on to explain, "You're constantly telling God, 'Thank you. I appreciate you. I praise you.' "

But listening, she emphasizes, is something altogether different. "We all know how to pray. But listening is the thing that we have not been trained to do, because even as kids we were always saying, 'Okay, Mommy, listen to me. All right, Daddy, listen to me. This is what I did today, blah, blah, blah, I, I, I.' "

"Listening takes patience," Yolanda continues. "It takes silence. Because God is not going to talk to you above the noise. He deserves more attention than that. So after you pray, turn the computer off, turn the television off . . . and just sit there and listen."

The chart-topping entertainer points out that very often answers to prayers do come quickly.

"But sometimes it takes time," she explains. "God will wait until you're finished with your stuff, until you're finished with your agendas, and whatever. And then He'll say, 'All right, now it's my turn.' That's when you've got to be ready to listen.

"And don't always expect a wordy message. You know, God could just say, 'You're doing good,' and that's all you'll get. That's all you get for that time with God.

"But even that can calm your soul, because you feel, 'Wow, I'm doing something God wants me to do.' You don't have to get pages and pages of stuff. Sometimes He'll just say, 'Keep on going.' You know, like today I was praying and meditating and then, all of a sudden, I heard those words."

Yolanda reveals that she prays regularly, but because of her hectic schedule, she has to be careful not to forget to set aside time to do so.

"Sometimes I'm in the midst of so much stuff, that I can forget the importance of God in my life," she candidly reveals. "And for as long as I've been walking with the Lord, that shouldn't happen. But you know, there are some days . . .

"So I have to keep a purpose in my mind: Look, I'm going to spend this time—even if it's just fifteen minutes, thirty minutes—whatever I can squeeze in. But Lord, don't think that I'm just trying to *squeeze* you in."

One method Yolanda uses to slow down and pay attention to God is to read Psalm 46, verse 10. "It's the one that says, Be Still and know that I am God," she relates.

"I read that Psalm today, because this was one of those days about let's hurry up and find new music for the new album; let's call all the people that you know and tell 'em to send all the music—all that kind of stuff.

"And I had to tell myself to slow down, and to be still and listen. It's not a question of making time, you want to have that time. So get into the habit of it, even if on some days you only have ten minutes."

She further suggests that there is nothing wrong with praying wherever you happen to be.

"You don't have to be in an office, or on your knees, or, you know, in a closet, or somewhere remote or isolated," she declares. "It can be in your car, on your way to wherever.

"Turn the car radio off, and make sure you don't get angry with the people who are driving in front of you or behind you," she laughingly adds. "And then concentrate on God."

Yolanda, who recently wed former New York Jets and Indianapolis Colts football player Timothy Crawford, nowadays is also kept busy on the lecture circuit as part of her ministry training.

"I teach, I do different women's conferences and things like that," she explains. "And when I talk to these groups I always give the message of my life, and how God took me from where I was to where I am today just by saying yes."

Many years have passed since Yolanda was instructed by her grandfather to act as a role model for her younger sisters and brothers. But the popular performer says she continues to behave in such a manner so as not to disappoint her many fans.

"When you're placed in a position of responsibility like I am, you have to act as a role model, like I did when I was a kid," she asserts. "You have no choice.

"I've been placed in this position by people who buy my records, and they believe what I'm saying. They want me to live the kind of life that God will be proud of. So you become a role model. It comes with the territory and you have to live responsibly."

Yolanda offers that she is always aware of being on center stage. "Some young girl, somewhere—she can be in Texas, she can be in California, she can be in New York—but she's watching every single thing that I wear, every single hairstyle I have, what I choose to do with my life.

"I mean, I got gifts from kids all over the United States when my husband and I got married. You know, you would think that these kids don't think about you that often. But they really care."

It is because she wants to continue to set an example for young people that Yolanda feels blessed to be performing gospel music.

"It's the kind of music that ministers in a God-fearing way," she proclaims. "Just look at the punk rockers, and the grunge people, who are always talking about dying and committing suicide. Look at their followers, and how they've influenced those kids negatively.

"Think of how many suicide pacts teenagers have been involved in because of some record. And it's the same thing with rap or gangsta rap. You know: Blow this person up, or, I got my gat with me. That is *negative* ministry. And I just don't believe in doing that."

Regarding the state of contemporary gospel, Yolanda is reluctant to criticize performers who have come under fire for being too radical in their approach to spiritual music.

"I've talked to many of the artists who are considered controversial," she relates. "And I know from talking to them that you just can't judge what somebody's doing at a glance. You have to sit down and talk to them, and find out exactly what it is that they're trying to do with this or that.

"And my view is that most of the people who are singing gospel music are trying to do what they believe God wants them to do. That's my personal opinion.

"Ten times out of ten everyone that I've talked to will say, 'This is the song that God gave me for the young people.' Or, 'This is the song that God gave me for people who are trying to find love in all the wrong places.'

"So I really believe that in every person—in every gospel artist—there is a desire to really please God, whether they are living for God and committed to God or not.

"If you listen to their entire album, I mean you'll hear God mentioned all through the album. So I don't criticize them. I don't want anybody trying to figure out what I'm doing with my music."

Yolanda acknowledges that over the years she has been subject to such criticism because of her use of jazz, gospel, and R&B in her music. What the veteran singer always tells such critics is that she is performing with spiritual sincerity.

"I've always believed that in spreading God's Word you should appeal to everybody—the oldsters, people who love pop music or jazz—*everybody,*" she says with emphasis.

"And look at Thomas Dorsey [considered the father of gospel music]. Everybody was saying, 'Get him outta here,' because he was playing blues. We just have to understand that change comes. The only thing that doesn't change is God."

Yolanda says her ultimate musical goal is to "cross barriers of age, race, and gender and reach people for Christ. I want to change people, free their hearts from hardness. I want to open up many doors to God. And I believe that God is opening up these doors through my music."

DOUG WILLIAMS

Photo by Gib Ford Photography, Jackson, MS

Doug has been a personal friend of mine for at least fifteen years. I think that Doug has a most unusual voice, and he's a wonderful support to his brother, Melvin. Doug is certainly no slouch when it comes to writing and producing gospel music, and he's been involved in the Christian experience for many, many years.

I highly rate Doug as an independent singer as well as a group player. He participates in most of the activities that are developed to promote gospel music in a very serious and outstanding way.

He is also very much involved with his record label, which indicates that he possesses the drive and knowledge that will help him to excel beyond just being an artist. He will move further into the field of ownership as well.

I think that Doug's personal testimonies concerning his relationship with Christ, and what the Lord has done to help him through many situations, are evident in the messages found in the many songs he has written.

Doug is certainly a soldier who is out there fighting God's battles. May God continue to bless his efforts.

Upset at the slow progress of his career, and hurting financially, Doug Williams remembers a point in his life when he and his brothers raised doubts about God's support of their musical ministry.

It was a trying period for the multi–Stellar Award–winning and Grammy-nominated Williams Brothers group, who were reared in a religious household and taught never to question the Lord.

"Things kind of started to shake us a little bit," the forty-one-year-old Blackberry Records artist recollects. "This was one of the times during the course of our career that things were going bad, and we were challenged."

The Mississippi native recalls how God spoke to him and his brothers through their father, a fiercely religious man, who had founded the group in 1960 when Doug and his brothers were just kids.

"He told us it was gonna be okay, if we just kept the faith. He would always give us encouragement and tell us to hang in there. So it didn't take long for us to get back to the basics."

His father's prediction turned out to be an accurate one. Since 1973, when the Williams Brothers caught fire with their first album, they have remained one of gospel's most sought-after groups.

"We've really been touched by God," Doug gratefully proclaims, "and we're spreading it to other people, too. I mean, continuing to bless people through our music—that's our goal."

Born the youngest child of Leon "Pop" and Amanda "Mom" Williams in the small town of Smithdale, Mississippi, located about a hundred miles from Jackson, Doug remembers being raised by parents who were God-fearing Christians.

"My dad was very involved in religion, and we were a very religious family living in this very, very small community where, basically, most of the people were related," he recalls.

"My folks brought us up in church, and church wasn't something where we had an option to go or not to go. I mean, it was mandatory that we had to go to church on Sunday."

Doug seems to enjoy reminiscing about his childhood in Smithdale, a dot-on-the-map farming community where both black and white farmers toiled side by side trying to eke out a living from the land.

"We grew up in the cotton fields," he laughingly relates. "We were picking cotton and pulling corn, and digging potatoes and peanuts. Just about everything we ate, we raised it on the farm there in Smithdale. There were six brothers in the family, all of us religious, and I was the youngest."

When Doug and his brothers weren't working in the fields, they could usually be heard practicing their singing. On Sundays, they could always be found at the Rosehill Missionary Baptist Church.

"It was a little white church sitting on a hill," he recollects. "I remember we were all excited about going to church. But that was just a normal thing on Sunday. I mean, that was something that was instilled in us since we were babies, and it was something that we always looked forward to."

Religion didn't end when the Sunday church service was over, Doug recalls. The sermon that the family heard in church that morning was always the subject of conversation over the dinner table. "That went on every Sunday without a doubt," he says with a laugh.

Besides religion, it was music that occupied the Williams household. Both of his parents sang gospel music. Doug's mother was a member of the church choir, while his father, when not farming, led his own gospel quartet.

"Everyone in our family sang," he relates. "My older brothers, my folks, we were all involved pretty much in music, one way or the other. My dad had an old group before we even got started; it was called "the Big Four Gospel Singers," and they were basically local."

Doug was only five years old when he began performing with his older brothers, who were known locally as "the Little Williams Brothers." But although gospel music was his favorite, it wasn't the only kind of music that Doug remembers listening to.

"Like all kids, I had an interest in other kinds of music," he explains. "I mean, me and my brothers were big fans of all different kinds of music, even though we were young kids and it really wasn't permitted for us to play any other kind of music in the house. But we would sneak and listen to Stevie Wonder, the Temptations, Aretha Franklin—people like that. We just liked their music."

Recognizing talent when he saw it, "Pops" Williams organized his kids as a group in 1960. As the brothers grew in talent, experience—and height—he changed the group's name to "the Sensational Williams Brothers." Later, they became known simply as "the Williams Brothers."

Doug describes his love of music as "just being part of me. I always wanted to be involved with my brothers in gospel music. It was just a natural part of me and I started singing with them when I was five.

"All the brothers went to the same junior high school where we sang together in the school choir, and the same high school. We could always be found singing in the school choirs. We sang at any opportunity we had."

Even after high school, the brothers continued to perform. Although they were locally popular, Doug remembers that he and his brothers wanted more than just local fame. He recalls it was at that point in their career when doubts began to set in about whether God really wanted them to expand their musical ministry.

Fueling those doubts were financial pressures. By now, some of his brothers were married, and the money the Williams Brothers were earning as a group simply was not sufficient to support them and their families.

"Things for us were really going bad back then," he reflects. "It was the 1970s and the group's faith was severely tested—you know, we weren't making any money.

"And some of us being married men, we had to take money home to our families. So that kind of started to shake my faith a little bit. We were all feeling discouraged."

It was an unusual state of mind for a family who "always stayed close in our walk with the Lord, and believed that God would bless us with our career in gospel music," the award-winning gospel star recalls.

"It was all about faith in God. There are challenges in everyone's life—I mean, there're some instances that can happen from time to time that will shake your faith, and this was one of those times."

Doug, who really loves and fears the Lord, quickly qualifies those remarks. "I think maybe we knew in the long run that God was gonna make it all right. So it really wasn't a loss of faith—just a little disappointment."

Whatever the thinking, the situation still was not a good one for the brothers, he recalls. "It took a lot of prayer for us to get through that time. I mean we would all come together, talk about what was going on, and pray about it."

Doug is convinced the group would have disbanded if it were not for the strong faith of his father, who persuaded his sons to stick with it.

"Our dad—he was our manager—would always give us encouragement. He'd pray with us. He'd say, 'Hang in there, 'cause God is gonna bring it out okay. Just keep that faith.' He was ministering to our hearts."

Although it was not easy for them to do so, the brothers did follow their father's advice. Doug recollects that it took three years of "trying to keep strong" before things finally did begin to turn around for the group as his father had prophesied they would.

"We just continued to believe that God wanted us to have this career. We believed He had blessed us with it," Doug declares. "So we stayed with the basics and tried to be grounded and rooted in our faith."

By 1973, the Williams Brothers had a record contract on the Songbird label. Their first album contained an instant hit song, and the record quickly climbed to the top of the charts. Coincidentally, the name of the hit song was "Jesus Will Fix It."

"It proved to us that if you keep faith with the Lord, in the long run He will make things right," Doug says with emphasis. "We just wouldn't let go of our faith. It was our love for God and what He's been in our lives that this was all about."

Since then, it has been a steady cruise on the top of the charts for the Williams Brothers, who over the years have recorded eighteen Top Ten albums, three Number One records, and have gone on to earn three Grammy nominations.

In 1986, the Williams Brothers received Stellar Awards for Best Traditional Gospel Group and Album of the Year, and since then have been the recipients of a drawerful of other honors.

The Williams Brothers have also performed at Madison Square Garden, Radio City Music Hall, the Grand Ol' Opry, and even at Carnegie Hall, as well as on numerous network television shows, including a CBS special honoring the late Dr. Martin Luther King Jr.

In 1991, the group formed its own record label, Blackberry Records, the first black owned and operated record label in the state of Mississippi that has major distribution.

As an individual artist, Doug has also gone on to earn a solid reputation for himself as one of the industry's finest writers, producers, and vocalists.

Since the 1970s, he has not only written and produced such popular gospel artists as the Mighty Clouds of Joy, the Canton Spirituals, and myself, but has also performed with the Mississippi Mass Choir, Yolanda Adams, Shirley Caesar, Amy Grant, and the Clark Sisters.

Already blessed with a successful recording career, Doug remembers another even more special blessing that he received one night in a Virginia hotel room.

"I had already been dedicated and trusted in God. Like I said, I'd been devoted to God since my childhood. But this was a whole new anointing," he testifies.

"This was back in 1988, and we had just finished a concert in Newport News, Virginia. When I got back to the hotel that night I felt that there was just something different . . . something about the night and about the way I felt. I knew it was different from anything that I had felt before."

Doug remembers lying awake in his room while his brothers down the hall were fast asleep. "It was about three or four o'clock in the morning, and all of a sudden I found myself on my knees praying.

"There were tears streaming from my eyes; there was just a whole different feeling. I think it was a calling upon my life at that point to really get more serious about my ministry; to really get closer to the Lord, and to really seek Him in everything that I tried to do. It was at this particular time that the Lord decided to deal with me."

Today, trying to put into words what happened to him in the early hours of that morning, Doug can offer no solid explanation as to why he was so touched by God. "I really don't know," he says with a shrug. "I think it was just, more or less, that God was ready for me at that moment to take what I was doing a lot more seriously."

When the thirty-year-old performer greeted his brothers later that day, he remembers feeling like an entirely reborn individual. "I had become a more dedicated Christian," he declares.

"I became more serious about my ministry, and really started trying to minister to the hearts and needs of other people. And I really got into paying my tithes, and things that I had been kind of letting go slack before. I was now just doing the things that a good Christian should do."

He recollects how the change in him was quickly noticed by his brothers. "They could tell there was something different about me. Then I shared the experience with them; I told them everything that had taken place that morning."

It was a joyful moment for him and his brothers, Doug recalls. "Everybody I told this to was happy about the situation because they all knew it was God's doing, that He had touched me."

His new spiritual anointing not only touched his brothers, but his wife, Levannah, and their children as well. "It really did have an effect upon my brothers and the rest of the members of the group," he submits. "They started to really seek the Lord more than they had before.

"And it spread to Levannah and my kids, too. They also sensed that there was something different about me, and that had a real positive effect on her. It kind of made her want to change some situations that were going on in her life."

Even today, his voice fills with excitement as he describes how his anointing impacted upon the Williams

Brothers' performance. "We became a more serious ministry," he declares.

"We were now ministering to the needs and hearts of people in our audiences, and they were touched. We've even had people say to us after a performance that they had been healed by just listening to our music, that it had a healing effect upon them."

Doug contends that it's the group's ability to infect their audiences with the spirit of the Lord that continues to fuel their popularity. "It makes me feel just great," the personable performer declares. "It lets me know that what I'm doing is not in vain . . . that our music is a ministry."

When Doug reflects upon all the blessings he has received since those early days of doubt, he admits that it sometimes takes his breath away. At such a moment, it is not unusual for the faith-driven star—who professes that his goal is "to become more like Jesus every day"—to fall upon his knees and thank God for His grace and generosity.

Trying to attain his goal is a daily challenge, Doug admits. "It's a constant challenge for me to be more like Jesus. It's something that you have to deal with on a daily basis, 'cause each day you're gonna be faced with a new situation.

"It's something that you have to stay prayerful about. You have to pray that you can handle situations, and hopefully handle them the way you feel that Jesus would handle them. It's a tough line to walk but a good line."

Doug, who, in addition to his singing duties, serves as president of his Blackberry Records label, advises anyone who wants to establish a closer walk with God to simply love and fear the Lord.

"I love God for what He's been in my life, but I also fear Him," the low-key, quiet, and humble artist attests. "I fear Him because you're supposed to fear Him. He is the Almighty . . . and we don't want to get on His bad side," he says with a laugh.

"It's important to fear the Lord because it's like a child coming up," the versatile performer explains. "Even though you don't want your child to be afraid of you, they should have some fear that if they do wrong then there's a punishment coming. So that's what I mean about fearing the Lord."

Doug offers that another important tool for capturing God's ear is prayer. "Get down on your knees and pray that God will speak to your heart, speak to your mind, speak to your spirit. Just really put faith and trust in Him that He will, and He will minister to your heart. And read the Book—that's always a good thing to do."

The inspired musical messenger discloses that prayer plays a vital role in his own life. "I pray on my knees, and I pray standing up," he reveals. "I pray while I'm driving my car, or riding on the tour bus. It can be anywhere. There's no certain time each day when I pray. It can be anytime."

Doug says his prayers are directed toward strangers as well as to members of his own family. "I pray for the needs of other people as well as my own," he proclaims. I also pray that He make me stronger every day. And I try to keep His anointing in my life by continuing to touch people in a positive way."

Looking ahead, the devoted Christian, family man, songwriter, producer, and record company executive hopes that the Williams Brothers ministry continues to grow. "We all pray that God will continue to carry our career," he declares.

"We pray that He'll allow us to continue touring, hopefully, for the next four or five years, and continue to bless people through our music. What we want is the ability to reach the masses with our ministry—that's our main goal. . . ."

SHIRLEY CAESAR

Photo by Matthew Barnes

Shirley is currently known as the "First Lady of Gospel Music." They called her that because she was the first lady on her record label to sing gospel, but that's not the only reason she deserves to have that title.

I consider Shirley one of the first ladies of gospel music because of her performance ability and how she interacts with her audiences in delivering her message. At times she even lays hands on people for healing and to help them overcome adversity and other problems.

She's a very energetic person. When she goes for it, she really goes for it. And she's very protective of herself, which is not bad. Whatever setting she's in, Shirley wants to make sure that she's recognized and that her ministry is effective to the point where people respond to her. And I think that's great!

Shirley had her first professional experience with the Caravans (they used to call her "little Shirley"), and after they disbanded she went ahead to develop her own group and ministry in a great way.

None of the other Caravans have been as successful as Shirley. The only one who ever came close to her was Dorothy Norton. We can definitely say that Shirley is a leader among the gospel singers. She is another general who leads the gospel army.

Her inspiring story is guaranteed to make you realize how very much this incredible artist has been touched by God.

*W*ith a fervency born of forty years onstage and an unfailing belief in God, Shirley Caesar's life has always been in spiritual high gear.

But despite her zeal for her ministry, there was a period just after the death of her beloved eighty-four-year-old mother when the eight-time Grammy Award winner allowed those gears to shift into low, and she even began to doubt some of the Scriptures.

"I was at the breaking point," declares the "First Lady of Gospel Music" with a surge of sadness in her voice.

It was just when the North Carolina native had reached her lowest point that the Lord stepped in to rejuvenate her lagging faith. And since that day the singer and evangelist has done all she can through her musical career and church ministry to praise God for taking her in His hand.

"He knew I was at a breaking point and He brought me through that," she joyfully proclaims. "He renewed me and revitalized my spirit, and I just praise the Lord for that."

At age fifty-nine, the remarkable gospel talent who first

began singing at age eight has never been clearer about her dedication to the Lord. Whether it's through her music, her preaching, or the outreach ministry that she operates for the poor and needy in her hometown of Durham, North Carolina, Shirley's message is a consistent one: Keep faith with the Lord.

"I keep hearing that God is dead," she says scornfully. "But if that's so, just answer me three questions: Who killed him? Who was the undertaker? And why wasn't I notified, because I'm His child and He's my father?"

That special feeling of connectedness to the Lord is something that the diminutive, faith-driven vocal powerhouse attests she has been aware of since the age of twelve, when twice in one week Shirley believes she was touched by God.

Those memories return the 1998 Grammy Award nominee to her days as a young girl growing up in Durham, where she was one of thirteen children raised by her widowed mother.

"I don't know if it was a poor neighborhood or not," Shirley asserts, "because everybody in the neighborhood was pretty much on the same level. If we were poor, none of us knew it.

"We were not rich by a long shot, that's for sure. In fact, as my sister Anne outgrew her clothes, they were handed down to me. But I never thought of myself as being poor."

The gospel star's memories of her father are fuzzy around the edges, because James Caesar died when she was only seven years old. What Shirley does remember about her father is how he instilled in her a love for gospel music.

"I got that love from my father," she declares in a mesmerizing voice. "He was a great gospel singer. He was like a gospel giant here in the Carolinas. He had a gospel quartet, and they would always win the competitions against other gospel quartets."

By the time she was eight, it was already apparent that Shirley had inherited much of her father's musical talent. At that young age she was already a regular at the local Mt. Calvary Holy Church, where the musically gifted youngster with the powerful voice could be heard belting out spirituals in the choir.

If Shirley wasn't performing with the choir, she could be found singing with one of her brothers' quartets. At age twelve, in an effort to support herself and her invalid mother, the youngster was already touring locally as a gospel soloist on weekends.

It wasn't only music that Shirley felt a close kinship with. Another centerpiece of her life was religion. "Both my parents were very religious, and from the time I got saved at twelve years old, I've always wanted to please the Lord," she submits.

She laughingly recalls that until that time, her walk with the Lord was a bit on the wild side. In fact, listening to Shirley talk about the trouble she got into as a youngster, the gospel great sounds as mischievous as Dennis the Menace.

"I wasn't perfect, but I was certainly striving for it, just like I'm doing today," she declares. "I'm still not perfect, but, let me tell you, every day of my life I try to get sweeter and sweeter—and I do!

"But back then I was a mischievous child. This little twelve-year-old girl was a mess. I'd go to school and talk back to the teachers; I got in little fights every day after school; I used to throw spitballs—today the kids throw knives—but I was throwing spitballs.

"And when the teacher would give us a test, I'd write the answer. And when she'd walk by us, I'd stick it on her back." Shirley pauses to emit a hearty laugh at that memory. "I used to love to break streetlights; I would shout in church because I saw the grown folks shouting . . . I'm telling you. I was really something."

But Shirley also remembers that she rarely got away with that kind of unruly behavior.

"Let me tell you. I got my share of whippings and everybody else's because of my behavior, and I deserved all of them. And every whipping that I got made me what and who I am today. And so I just praise the Lord for that."

All her acting out came to an end when Shirley accepted Jesus into her life, she recalls. "I went through a lot of changes when I got saved, and I remember exactly when that happened.

"It was in February and I got saved on Valentine's night. I remember that we had a revival meeting going on, and it had been going on for about two weeks. And I had been going with some of my older brothers and sisters every single night for one whole week.

"And then in the second week—on that Tuesday night—I came into the church and I sat in the back. And while I was sitting there, a lady by the name of Mother Mildred Reed, she got up and sang a song with the choir."

Shirley recites a verse from the song, which she still remembers:

> In shady green pastures,
> so rich and so sweet,
> God leads His dear children
> Alone, where the cool waters
> flow. . . .

Not only did the words to the song deeply affect her, but everyone else in the church, too, the gospel star recalls. "Well, I sat there and people were feeling the presence of the Lord all around me.

"And, you know, I don't care who you are. If you come into the presence of the Lord often enough, you're gonna feel something. And I was listening to that song and I started feeling something.

"Then the preacher—her name was Dorothy Ilam, and she was the one who inspired my ministry—got up and preached. And afterward, she made the altar call. And I was sitting right back there in the back of the church with my brother, and I literally heard a knock at the door of my heart."

Shirley pauses, reliving that moment in her mind's eye. She continues with excitement in her voice.

"And in my spirit it looked like Jesus was standing in front of me saying: 'Shirley, if you open the door of your heart, I'll come in.' He said, 'Now, the knob is on the inside. You've got to be willing to open that door if you want me to come in.'

"And before I knew it, I jumped up out of my seat, ran to the front of the church, pushed my way past everybody—they were all on their knees—and fell prostrate in the presence of the Lord.

"And I just cried: 'Come into my heart, Lord, come into my heart.' And I was jumping up and down, and running around, and crying out. Then I fell back down on my knees.

"And when I got up I was saved. When I got up I was a changed person. I wasn't that mischievous girl anymore. When I was down on my knees He sanctified my life—He cleaned my life. I didn't even have to ask Him for forgiveness."

The gospel star can still remember walking out of the church that morning and feeling as if she had been reborn. What she didn't realize is that God was not quite through with her yet.

"I was very anxious to be back in church, so I left my house real early the next Thursday night and stopped off at this church woman's house—I can't even remember her name.

"She was a tiny woman, about four feet tall, and she was from the Church of God of Prophecy. She was a very religious woman. I stopped by her house to tell her how I'd gotten saved on Tuesday night."

As Shirley related her story, the elderly woman gazed deeply into the young girl's eyes. Shirley recalls feeling as if the woman was gazing into the very depths of her soul.

"Do you want the baptism of the Holy Ghost?" the woman asked.

"Yes," Shirley replied, not knowing exactly what to expect.

"Well, that old mother had me kneel down, and she laid her hands on my head. And she started praying for me. I lay down on the floor and this little lady straddled me. She lay across my waist, and she said: 'Shirley, God has a call and a plan for your life. Receive ye the Holy Ghost.' "

Even to this day, the gospel great remains awestruck by that woman's accurate prophecy. "I mean I was just twelve years old at the time and I didn't know that God was going to bring me to where I am today.

"But she knew exactly what was gonna happen to me. She said, 'God's got a plan, God's got a plan for your life. God's gonna use you.' And she laid her hand on me, she straddled me, and she said: 'Receive ye the Holy Ghost.' And here I am, forty years later—even longer than that—and God has brought everything that she said into fruition."

Shirley's rise to national prominence began in 1958, when she was invited to join the Caravans by Albertina Walker. Getting that job, however, took a bit of "finagling," she recalls.

The Caravans, at the time, were in town doing a Sunday afternoon concert. Shirley and a friend went to see the performance, and the young singer remembers thinking how much the group could benefit from a fourth voice.

"I couldn't get Albertina to pay any attention to me that day," she recalls. "So when they played another show nearby, I managed to get on the stage and did a solo for her between the acts."

Instead of becoming angry, Albertina was so impressed by the young girl's voice that she offered Shirley a position with the group right there on the spot.

Shirley remained with the Caravans until 1966, eventually taking over as lead singer from Albertina Walker. During those years the teenager began to develop her own preaching style, which eventually led to her decision to become an evangelist.

By 1972, the vocal powerhouse had formed her own gospel group: the Shirley Caesar Singers. Wanting to do more for the needy, she also organized the Shirley Caesar Outreach Ministries in Durham. The ministry provided food, clothing, and counseling to the destitute in the area.

Shirley recollects that the idea to form her outreach program came while attending a convocation in Chicago.

"I was living in Chicago at the time, and I got to hear some marvelous preachers. It encouraged me to start my own outreach ministry to help those in need by bringing in preachers to give spiritual sustenance and economic benefit."

The accomplished gospel star says she is more proud of her ministry than the many awards she has earned over the years. "He's used me to touch other people with this ministry," she declares of a program that has literally helped thousands of needy people over the years.

Shirley recalls that the ministry once helped to save the life of somebody very special to her: her own thirty-seven-year-old niece, who was suffering from a longtime cocaine addiction when she turned to the ministry for help.

"Cassietta had hit rock bottom," Shirley relates, "but she gave her heart to the Lord, and God set her free. I know that if He can turn her life around—she had spent most of her life as a crack addict—then he can do it for anybody else."

Although her life continued in spiritual high gear, there was a painful time when the phenomenal singer and songwriter faced a challenge to her faith, the death of her beloved mother.

"When my father died I was too young to really know that much about him," she offers. "But my mama—I just felt that Mama would never die. I felt that she would be with us always. We were very, very close. I took care of my mom from the time that I was twelve years old until I laid that empty house to rest.

"I had never backed away from the Lord, but I found myself really questioning certain Scriptures during that period. He said, 'If you will have the faith the size of a grain of mustard seed, you can ask me for anything.' And when my mother became ill I was asking Him with all my heart and soul to spare her life."

Shirley's voice cracks with emotion as she continues her testimony. "I found myself, in a sense, perturbed— not angry—but somewhat disappointed that He didn't save her even though I had always had trust and faith in Him. I wanted Him to spare her.

"But what I didn't understand was that my mother was eighty-four years old when she passed. It didn't dawn on me then how many people lose their mothers in child-birth, and how blessed I was to have her live so long."

Instead, all Shirley could focus on were her impassioned pleas to the Lord for Him to spare her mother's life. When her prayers failed, the gospel artist was distraught. "I became severely depressed. It was a moment when I faced the greatest challenge to my faith," she declares.

Today, the multiple Grammy Award winner believes she made it through that period only because God spoke to her through her husband of fourteen years, Bishop Harold Williams.

"I remember that right after my mother passed—even before the funeral—my husband took me by the hand and walked me through sleet and rain here in the city. He quoted victory Scriptures and he made me repeat them after him."

As she did so, Shirley recollects how the constant repetition of those Scriptures began to have an uplifting effect upon her. "Not every Scripture in the Bible is a victory Scripture," she explains. "But there are some Scriptures where He is talking directly to Israel.

"I just reached for those Scriptures. I pulled out the ones where I felt the Lord was talking to me and concentrated on those. And the more I would do that, the better I began to feel.

"I continued to keep my faith by quoting those Scriptures. The Lord brought me through this and I soon got over my depression. His Word just began to strengthen me—it just uplifted my spirit."

Shirley also began to understand that instead of doubting the Lord, it was gratitude that she should have expressed because God had given her mother such a long life.

"The Lord just began to speak to my spirit and said, 'I gave her to you. I let her live longer than the promise.' The Bible says the promise is threescore and ten—seventy—and she would have been eighty-five that January nineteenth. So He had blessed me. I just wasn't able to understand that at the time."

Having emerged with her faith in God intact through such a painful experience, Shirley, today, is dedicated to helping others get through their own suffering without turning away from the Lord.

"There's so much tragedy in the world today," she declares. "I want to make every individual feel that God is talking to Him or Her and that the Lord will get them through."

She counsels anyone who is feeling depressed to count their blessings and be grateful for what they have. "Anytime we can wake up healthy in the morning, and drive past the cemetery, we ought to count our blessings," she asserts.

"We can spend so much time worrying over little things when there are people every day dealing with life and death issues. We need to think on the goodness of Jesus and put total confidence in Him."

Looking back over her life, Shirley admits with heartfelt honesty that she is not really certain why she has been so blessed by God.

"He could've chosen any one of the twelve children and given them this career," she submits. "But, instead, he used me. The years have been good to me and the Lord has been good to me. All I can say is thank you, Jesus, thank you, Lord."

It is certainly not an understatement for a performer who, in her forty-year career, has recorded thirty albums and has been nominated for sixteen Grammys—more than any gospel artist in history.

When she is behind the pulpit at the Mount Calvary Word of Faith Church, in Raleigh, North Carolina, where she serves as pastor, Shirley's sermons all focus on her unfailing belief in God.

She constantly emphasizes to her congregation that in order to feel God's presence, it's important to "love Him, and Him alone. You must love Him to the extent that you'll put nothing before your prayer time, your Bible study time, your church time.

"And you must always remember the ABC's of salvation. A—admit that you need the Lord. B—believe that God is God, and that God gave us His son Jesus to come into this cruel world, to die for us so that we can live again.

"And C—commit. Once you believe, then commit. Commit your ways, your life, your heart over to the Lord Jesus Christ. When you do these ABC's, you'll become a brand-new creature in Christ Jesus."

Commitment is quite important to the singer and evangelist, who believes that all her efforts must be directed at the Lord. Shirley relates that over the years her commitment to gospel music has been frequently tested, particularly by secular record companies who keep dangling lucrative financial offers before her eyes.

"It's not really been such a difficult decision to say no. They were making all these claims about turning me into a big star," she laughingly relates, "but I would have to sing R&B or rock 'n' roll. They were telling me how they could make me bigger than Mahalia Jackson or Sam Cooke.

"I told them that I believed gospel music was God's music, that it speaks of Him. I said my love for the Lord wouldn't allow me to sing R&B. I finally said that the only way I'd sing rock 'n' roll is if they let me rock for Jesus and roll for God. After that, they left me alone. I wasn't going to yield to changing my music."

The faith-driven gospel star adds there is another reason why she will not perform secular music. It has to do with a wish from her dying mother. "Just before Mama passed, I had done some restrained, pop sort of albums," she relates. "One day my mama called me over to her bed and said, 'I want the old Shirley back.' "

With tears in her eyes, Shirley promised her mother she would never again stray from her gospel music heritage. "My mama got a brand-new daughter. Right after that I came out with 'Hold My Mule,' and that returned me right back to my gospel roots."

Originally released in 1987, the song combined music, ministry, and message delivered in a special "Caesarized" way. The record has since become a gospel music classic.

It also helped to launch her on a career in which this remarkably multitalented entertainer has garnered three gold records, thirteen Stellar Awards, and fifteen Dove Awards in addition to her multiple Grammy honors.

Looking ahead, the gospel music perennial, who is still one of the industry's most heralded performers, states that she is not finished pushing the limits of her musical talent or her pastoring skills.

"Sure it's tough to keep all these things going in my life," she concedes, "but if I gave up my ministry for singing, I'd get a whipping from the Lord. I believe that singing and preaching go together like ham and eggs. So I want the world to know that Shirley Caesar is pastoring in Raleigh, North Carolina."

Shirley proudly adds that her church—located just around the corner from Shaw University, where Shirley graduated magna cum laude in 1983—had only forty congregants when she first took over the pastoral duties there.

Nowadays, the congregation is growing at such a rapid pace that land has been purchased to construct a new, thirteen-hundred-seat church building. Shirley, who takes no salary for her church work, is currently trying to raise $500,000 to break ground for the new building.

"I want this little church to speak out. I want to see this church sponsoring a drug ministry, a singles ministry, and a teen ministry," she declares. "I want to see a program going to help alcoholics. And I'd like to have a huge youth program going here. Most of all, I want to touch the hurting and help people.

"I want people who are hurting to know that all they have to do is just get up, straighten themselves out, and keep on going. And you can't do that without God in your life."

KIRK FRANKLIN

Photo by Greg Allen

Little did I know when Vickie Mack Laatillade came to me backstage in Atlanta, Georgia, while we were taping our 1994 gospel program and asked me to give her artist, Kirk Franklin, an opportunity to perform, that Kirk would go on to be one of the most sought-after artists in the business. I thank God for the opportunity to have presented him to the masses first.

I now know Kirk personally. He is all of that! When we have the opportunity to get together, he treats me like I'm his father—and I love it, especially since I'm old enough to be his grandfather! It's good to be part of a success situation.

Kirk is very sensitive about his music and its position in the Christian gospel music arena. He appears to want to please all the elements that surround him.

I really began to discover some of Kirk's other talents when I invited him to attend an international gospel event in Barbados, West Indies. His performance, without his background group, The Family, was excellent. When he sat down at the keyboard and began to express himself, he included the audience and the other groups. It was truly a blessed and wonderful tour.

The Lord chose Kirk to continue to spread His word throughout the world. Kirk is certainly in the front of the army of gospel music performers who are leading God's battle. His youthful appeal, his marriage, his love for people and his work will continue to forge new directions and opportunities for others seeking a similar platform.

His story of coming off the mean streets to become a general in the Lord's army will certainly lead you to realize that Kirk Franklin is touched by God!

$\mathcal{A}$s a teenager, gospel music superstar Kirk Franklin was more involved in spreading mayhem in the ghetto streets of Fort Worth, Texas, than the Word of the Lord.

It took the gun-related death of one of Kirk's friends for the troubled fifteen-year-old to reach out for God's hand. Since then, the 1998 Grammy winner has broken barriers, crossed music boundary lines, and achieved a success previously unknown to other gospel artists.

Although success is certainly his for the taking, Kirk insists that it isn't awards and Number One records that matter the most to him. Instead, the accomplished twenty-seven-year-old singer, songwriter, and minister declares that he is striving to win over more people for the Lord.

"I never want my purpose to be gold albums," the Dove and Stellar Award–winning Gospo Centric recording artist insists. "I'm just grateful to say that through God I've been able to touch so many lives. I want to continue to offer people an opportunity to accept Christ."

Born Kirk Smith in Fort Worth, Texas, the real miracle in his life is that the highly acclaimed performer is even around today to sing the Lord's praises.

Abandoned by his teenage mother when he was three, and never knowing his father, Kirk gravitated to the streets, where trouble always brewed and run-ins with the cops were not unusual for the youngster and his friends.

Kirk isn't exactly proud of his gang-banging ways back then, but he does want people to understand why he behaved in such a manner. "It was an acceptance thing, you know," he recently explained in an interview with *VIBE* magazine.

"I was tryin' to be accepted—you know, doin' anything I could for people to like me," the acclaimed performer says of his former lifestyle. "So I did whatever it took—you know, gettin' carried away in the clubs and bein' the one that always buys the liquor.

"I was smoking pot, drinking, disrupting school, hanging out with a bad crowd, and wantin' to be a gangster with all the other brothers because I didn't want them to think I was soft—although I was."

That softness has always been part of the acclaimed singer's personality, as much as he once tried to hide it. "I wanted to show that I wasn't no punk," he asserts in the interview. "Everybody was smokin' and drinkin' and stuff, and I wanted to be down with 'em."

But that gentle side existed nonetheless, partly because of the influence on his life of his sixty-four-year-old great-aunt, Gertrude Franklin, who adopted the youngster when he was four.

A devout churchgoer, it was his elderly aunt, whom Kirk always fondly refers to as "my mother," who taught her ward about Jesus, self-respect, and the importance of respecting others.

"That's somethin' I guess I never forgot," he asserts. "She taught me everything that I still consider important.

On Sunday mornings she made sure I was in church. She made sure I had a proper Baptist upbringing."

Gertrude not only made certain that Kirk attended church, but also encouraged his musical ability. Recognizing that her adopted son had talent, she prompted Kirk to begin taking piano lessons even before he started school.

The gospel star still remembers how he and his aunt would often go out on Saturdays collecting tin cans and newspapers for recycling. With the money that they earned, Gertrude would pay for those lessons. "She really sacrificed for me," he asserts. "I thank God for the opportunities she gave me."

At seven Kirk was already showing so much musical promise in church, that he was offered a record deal by a small gospel label. His aunt, however, would not permit it because of his young age.

That talent continued to flourish. At age eleven, Kirk beat out the adults for the position of minister of music at the Dallas-based Mt. Rose Baptist Church, where he sang, composed music, and led the adult choir. "I was leading a chorus with people sixty and older," he laughingly recalls. "Can you imagine an eleven-year-old tellin' his elders they were singing wrong?"

But despite such loving attention from his aunt, and what looked like the start of a promising musical career, Kirk still opted for the role of the bad boy.

"I was always a moody kid," he relates. "In the house it was just me and an older woman. When I got around my peers, I was just buck wild, because I wanted to be a kid, you know?"

There were other reasons, he recalls, that he tried to act like a tough guy: one of them was being teased as a "church boy" by his teenage friends. "See, when I was comin' up," he says in the magazine interview, "the guys in church were considered gay, sissies. So whatever it took for me to prove that I wasn't that, that's what I did." Kirk went on to tell the *VIBE* reporter, "Man, when I was in high school, I was called gay so much that I used to wake up in the morning crying and begging my mother not to send me to school. It got to the point that one morning, she didn't force me."

That kind of teasing and the fact that he was also made fun of because of his height (today Kirk stands at five foot four), often resulted in his aggressive behavior and his "gettin' into a lot of fights."

Reflecting back, Kirk can still recall how he never felt quite right about his behavior. Not only was he disappointing his mother, but he felt hypocritical singing in church on Sundays after a night of drinking and smoking.

"I knew what I was doing was wrong, but when you're tryin' so hard to be accepted, you don't really think about the consequences of what you're doin'," he explains.

"So I was still doin' the marijuana and hanging out at a nightclub near where I lived. I was drinkin', gettin' into fights, and gettin' into trouble with the cops. I was always one of these tough neighborhood brothers."

Kirk's life continued in that confused manner until his eyes were opened by the death of a close friend—an incident, the gospel music superstar recalls, that made him realize for the first time that he was not invincible.

It was the summer of 1985 when seventeen-year-old Eric Pounds was accidentally shot and killed. As he was reaching for his parents' gun, the weapon fell from a closet shelf and discharged.

Kirk, then fifteen, remembers how much the news of his friend's death frightened him. It was time, he decided, to try and straighten his life out. "Man, it woke me up," he exclaims. "That was the first time anybody young who was close to me had ever died. So you know, it scared me.

"And when it happened, it was like everything that I read in church—I'd been around church a lot—it was kind of like, 'Boom,' you know, this life and death thing is real and you're gonna have to make some decisions."

Kirk remembers being at home when he first heard about his friend's death. He further recalls walking into his mother's den, falling on his knees, and praying for deliverance. "I'd been goin' to church all my life, but my heart wasn't in it," he offers.

"But that all changed now. I realized that what I had been doing was wrong. I think God was touchin' me; He was showin' me what could happen to me if I continued with this gang-banging lifestyle. God was showin' me that I *wasn't* invincible.

"And I just got on my knees, and I talked to the Lord: 'Lord, my life's not right with you. I haven't accepted you as my Savior. I want to give my life to you and I want you to forgive me for all my sins. I accept you as my Savior. I believe you are the Son of God and I want to be saved.' "

There was no instant response from the Lord to his prayers. "No, it wasn't like a movie," he says, smiling. "There was no big, bright white light that comes from the ceiling or nothin' like that. There was just a peace that I felt. There was a peace that I got.

"Things changed slowly for me. It wasn't an overnight thing. But I started givin' up things one by one. The first thing that left me was smokin' weed—just like that. And then I stopped drinkin'. Even my appetite for clubs slowly left me."

The changes he was undergoing began to be noticed by his friends and his mother, Kirk recalls. "My friends sensed it in me and my mom sensed the change in me— she sensed everything about me," he adds with a laugh. "And she praised the Lord for it because she was a churchgoing woman and she always prayed for it."

Although, today, Kirk believes without any doubt that God touched him at that time of his life, he can offer no real explanation as to why he was singled out.

"I really have no idea, man," the highly successful entertainer asserts. "All I know is that I was the last person to deserve it. I mean, man, if anybody should be lost it should've been me. Maybe it has something to do with predestination. All I know is that God ministered to me."

Although there were a few false starts, Kirk recalls that, for the most part, he managed to steer a fairly straight course in his new walk with the Lord.

"Yeah, I took some more blows to my head and there were a couple more scars," he relates. "But there was a lot more sensitivity in how I was relating to the Lord. And there was also God's grace and my mother's prayers."

Kirk now found himself spending more time in church than on street corners. He was also studying the Scriptures, and focusing more on his music.

"I'd been in the church all my life doin' the music," he relates. "And then I gave my life to the Lord at fifteen, and I started preachin'. And so between fifteen and seventeen I really started gettin' serious about my music. I wanted to spread a message about God's love. I wanted to tell people all about God's power and have the music move them at the same time."

It wasn't until Kirk was nineteen that he had an opportunity to do so. He met Milton Biggham, a Savoy Records producer, who was beginning to form the Dallas–Fort Worth Mass Choir.

After listening to a demo that the teenager had sent him, Biggham, a thirty-seven-year veteran of the gospel scene, who would later go on to found the award-winning Georgia Mass Choir, asked Kirk if he would compose some songs for the ensemble.

Kirk quickly agreed, putting together a seventeen-member entourage composed mostly of his friends. He named the group The Family, because "it gave me the sense of family I always wanted," Kirk declares. "These were people I knew and trusted, people who knew me back when I had nothin'."

Soon afterward, the exceptionally talented singer and his ensemble were offered a recording contract with the prestigious Savoy Records label.

Then another opportunity presented itself. Kirk remembers receiving a phone call one afternoon from an upstart Los Angeles label—Gospo Centric—that would later become one of the industry's powerhouse labels.

On the line was Vickie Mack Lataillade, a former RCA executive, who started the label with money she borrowed from her father's post office pension. Vickie had heard one of Kirk's earlier rough demos and was impressed by the raw talent on that tape.

"She said she couldn't pay me as much as my present label, but she told me she'd work longer and harder to promote me," Kirk recollects. He remembers praying for guidance for several days, and then signing with the new label. The first album that Kirk and his group released in 1993 sold in excess of a million copies.

Since then, Kirk and his "family" have gone on to become one of the most successful gospel groups of the past decade, winning Dove and Stellar awards and a 1998 Grammy along the way.

In his four years with the group, Kirk has produced nothing short of a revolution in gospel music—and has also generated much criticism—because of his unorthodox approach to the genre.

With his hip-hop generation trademark look that includes a cap worn backward, baggy jeans, and tennis shoes, Kirk has become the musical and spiritual leader of a new breed of youthful gospel artists.

"Music must become all things to all people in order to win them for Christ," he says in response to the flak that he has received from gospel music purists who believe he has taken praise music too far.

"Generation X doesn't want to hear from the reverend behind the pulpit, or go to any Bible conferences," he contends. "So we need to go about getting the message to them in another way. That doesn't mean my way isn't godly just because I'm not using the same tools they're using. The bottom line is to reach the kids too."

Kirk believes his unique gospel music ministry is already reaping spiritual rewards. "We have a base of young people who are sending in fan mail," he offers.

"We've already received over four thousand pieces of mail. These kids have gotten back in the church and made commitments and rededicated their lives. We've been real examples to these young people."

Although Kirk's life might read like something straight out of a movie script—tough inner-city kid from the ghetto streets of Fort Worth goes on to become a music star—there have been many rewrites along the way.

Last year, for example, the faith-driven singer who has put religious music on the pop charts as well as the gospel charts suffered a near-fatal fall while performing on a darkened stage in Memphis, Tennessee.

Kirk landed on his head in an orchestra pit located ten feet below, and lay unconscious in the hospital for several hours. Worried doctors thought he might die or have permanent spinal or brain damage.

Miraculously, the gospel star suffered only two brain contusions, bouncing back six weeks later to give a performance at the twelfth Annual Stellar Gospel Music Awards. "I'm just very blessed," he declares. "I don't even remember anything that happened to me."

Kirk scoffs at accusations that his injury was punishment from God for his hip-hop approach to sacred music. "I don't think of it as a punishment but a transition," he offers. "It was ordained to happen and it made me feel like I had died and moved on to a higher level.

"That was a graduation," he continues. "Every night I'd preach Jesus is real. But when I fell and I was lying there in a pool of blood, I saw that Jesus was real."

Although Kirk submits that he has experienced various challenges to his faith over the years, he attests that none have been greater than what he is now undergoing while rehearsing for a new television comedy series.

He contends that the Hollywood lifestyle is not conducive to people of faith, and that it is often difficult for him to function as a spiritual person in such an environment.

"That's why my being in the type of situation I'm in right now is a challenge to my faith every day, I mean more than at any other time in my life," he declares. "It's a greater challenge than anyone would think.

"I'm a gospel artist and a church boy, and this is an industry and a city that's all about self, not about God or spirituality. What's important here is, 'I'm hot, I'm number one, I'm on top, praise me, glorify me, I'm better than you, I'm better looking, I got a good nose job, I've got a good complexion' . . . you know. I mean, this is a very vain and self-glorious type business that I find myself in."

Kirk, who is an ordained minister, laughingly relates that he manages to cope with the situation by "keeping my knees white and trying to keep my mouth shut.

"I'm from the church and I represent the church for whatever reason God has me here. And I want to make sure that wherever I am that I'm the same. And that can sometimes be a challenge."

Kirk further emphasizes that it's prayer, not Hollywood parties, that he attends to while completing the taping of his forthcoming series. "I pray every day, but there's no set ritual," he explains.

"It may just be getting out of bed and sayin', 'I love you, thank you, Lord.' Or it could be while I'm in the shower. It could be while I'm on the way down to the gym or in my car.

"It's not a ritual because what happens in a ritual is you do it once, and the rest of the day you don't do it at all, instead of trying to make it part of your daily routine. That's what I try to do. I try very hard to make prayer part of my daily routine."

But although Kirk is deeply committed to the spiritual life, he candidly discloses that his walk is a far from perfect one. "I'm still learnin' and I'm still growin' and still makin' mistakes," he admits. "And I'm always tryin' to learn from the mistakes I've made."

His advice for others who also want to strengthen their own spiritual walk is to stop trying to please people. "Stop tryin' to impress people. Stop trying' to do it yourself—this super saint stuff. Just let God have His way in your life. Then your life will be so much more peaceful."

He also has a special piece of advice for youngsters who are caught up in the gang-banging scene that he was once part of: "Don't get caught up in that," he declares. "Everybody wants to be a gangsta. Everybody wants to be this big rapper. Everybody wants to drive the Mercedes and all that stuff. Don't get caught up. Because all that is only for a moment."

Looking toward the future, Kirk, who was recently married and is living in Texas with his new wife, Tammy, a former member of the R&B group Ashanti, and their three children, says he wants to continue to reach people through his musical ministry.

"I want to spread the gospel wherever I can," he declares, "especially outside the church walls and to young people. I want to go as far as God wants me to go. I'm just trying to stay focused.

"I'm trying to have a vision of stomping out the devil. And I pray that God will use me to usher in a breed of Christian artists who will be good stewards over the vocation to which they were called. I want to use this wonderful gift that God has given me to be a good steward with it."

DOTTIE PEOPLES

Photo by Troy Plota

Dottie is a special person. When I first heard her sing, she was a soloist in her church choir in Atlanta, Georgia. I didn't follow Dottie's career much at that time and was quite surprised and pleased when she was introduced to the gospel community via her recording. I immediately began to take notice. Before long, Dottie's ministry had become very recognizable around the nation—and the rest is history.

To some, it might seem that Dottie came a long way in a short period of time. But Dottie came up at the right time to fill a space that was void for a short while: traditional gospel with a female voice. Her down-home style was just right. Her wonderful vocals mixed with a warm personality propelled her to a positive position in the gospel music industry.

Dottie is a family lady. She was pleased to introduce me to her mother and some of her other family members. They were all very proud of Dottie and supported her every move. That situation, in addition to her tremendous talent, created a soft spot in my heart for her.

Dottie's experience traveling and representing Jesus on a regular basis is strengthening her fan base as well as her record sales. Another thing you might want to know about Dottie is that she has established the fact that she loves to wear gowns. Whatever the event, look for Dottie to be in her gown. She is developing her look and style.

I feel that Dottie has what it takes to become a special witness for Christ and to save souls. Dottie Peoples— another soldier who is touched by God.

$\mathcal{A}$lthough the Stellar Award–winning performer always believed that her vocal talents would someday be dedicated to serving the Lord, what Dottie didn't anticipate was becoming lost on her spiritual path somewhere along the way.

The Ohio native recalls straying from that path during a period of her life when she found herself singing jazz in nightclubs rather than the worship music she loved and grew up with in church.

All that dramatically changed one Sunday morning when the award-winning vocalist, while auditioning for a church choir, believes she was touched by an angel!

Since that day, the highly acclaimed performer has never set foot in a jazz club again. "From then on I did what I always wanted to do," she declares. "I just wanted to sing for the Lord and see other people healed through my singing. And that's what I did."

Reminiscing about her childhood in Dayton, Ohio, Dottie recalls that her great-grandmother, Solinia Golsby—to whom she gives much of the credit for her religious upbringing—always had faith that the youngster would someday grow up to be a gospel artist.

The eldest of ten children, Dottie and her sister Juanita were always her great-grandmother's favorites, and would spend their school vacations with Solinia at her home in Birmingham, Alabama.

"She started getting us when I was seven or eight," Dottie relates. "And she would always look at me and tell me she knew I was gonna be a singer. She said when I was in church I'd always sit on the edge of the seat and just look at all the ladies leading the songs in the choir."

Although just a youngster, Dottie says even then she sensed that her great-grandmother's prophecy would someday come true. "I'd always tell her I wanted to be just like Mahalia Jackson. I always talked to her about being a singer."

It was during those summer months in Birmingham that the two sisters received much of their religious training—something that their own mother was too busy to do while trying to raise ten kids, Dottie recalls.

Her father also did not have much time to spend on his children's religious training, the gospel star relates. "He was a hardworking man who held down a series of jobs at General Motors. Until they raised him to a higher position, he would work two or three jobs to support the family."

With her great-grandmother, however, it was an entirely different matter.

"Mama was too busy having babies," she says, laughing, "although she always found a way to go to church. But with Grandma, we'd go to Sunday school, regular church services. I mean, she had us in church all day and all night."

At the small Birmingham church Dottie attended, it was the gospel music more than the services that attracted her. "I'd feel the passion and the praise to God," she declares. "I was entranced by it. I felt it was my music."

Dottie recalls that her neighborhood was not a poor one. "We weren't poor and we weren't rich. My daddy worked real hard to make *sure* we weren't poor, that we had decent things and everything."

By age ten, Dottie was already taking steps that would one day make her great-grandmother's prophecy come true. On Sundays the musically gifted youngster could always be found singing with the young adult choir.

"I just always wanted to sing," she states. "I believe it was God's gift to me. And I thought singing gospel music was the sweetest thing. I mean," she says with a laugh, "to see those ladies up there singing, and bawling, and all that."

If God blessed Dottie with a beautiful singing voice, there was another gift that He bestowed upon her when she was just ten years old: a visitation. The impact of that special moment on her life was so dramatic that Dottie felt compelled to share it on her 1996 release, *You Can Count on God.*

That momentous occasion began as a result of a dream that her great-grandmother had, one that greatly disturbed the elderly woman.

"I remember that we were in the country with her when she brought us to her room. Grandma said she had brought us up there that summer for a particular reason.

"Grandma told me and my sister Juanita that she had this dream. In it, she was going to heaven, and my sister and I were going to hell. She was going up and we were going down."

When Solinia finished relating her vision, Dottie can still remember how the elderly woman fiercely locked eyes with her and her sister.

"It's time for you two to get on the mourner's bench," Solinia said in a voice that breached no rebuttal.

Dottie recalls exchanging puzzled glances with her sister. "As kids, we didn't know nothing about the mourner's bench. In these little country churches, it's the first bench up front, right in front of the preacher."

Then her great-grandmother barked another order.

"You all are gonna get real religion this summer. There's not gonna be no whole lot of playing."

It was not happy news, she recalls. "My birthday was every summer—it's in August. And Grandma said, 'No cake, no ice cream, no birthday party. You're gonna pray and ask God to save you this summer.' "

And her great-grandmother was as good as her word, Dottie recollects. "I remember that we went out to the country with my great-grandmother to this old-time camp meeting—you know, it was done the *old* way. Me and my sister, we sat there. They prayed, but we really didn't know what was going on. We were there for a week.

"When the week was up, I told my grandma that I didn't feel anything," she recalls, laughing. "And then I told her that Saturday was supposed to be my birthday party."

Dottie remembers that her statement did not reach appreciative ears. She said, 'You're not having a party. You're still gonna pray and ask God to save you.' God had put it into her heart to get us in church because of that dream."

Dottie tried to get a last word in. "I asked my grandma, I said, 'Well, Big Mama, how do I know when I got religion?' She said, 'You ask the Lord for a sign.' "

The statement perplexed her. What sign could she ask from the Lord? Then it suddenly came to her. "Well, I'd always been a sleepyhead," she laughingly relates. "I didn't like to get up early.

"So I didn't know no better than to say: 'Lord, if I got it, wake me up in the morning early.' Dottie, again, laughs at that memory. "I knew that if He got me up early, that meant something.

"And I went to bed that night and I prayed. I asked God: 'If you've touched me, and I've got religion, I want you to wake me up before the rooster crows.' And that morning I woke up, and I looked out the window, and then the rooster said . . ." Dottie mimics the crowing of a rooster, chuckling as she does so.

"So I didn't tell nobody. I went to church with my great-grandmother that Sunday morning and I didn't say a word. I sat on the mourner's bench. I went in real quiet, and my sister was also sitting up there. We sat there—my great-grandmother put us there—and when the preacher held out his hand, my sister looked at me. She said, 'What are you gonna do?' "

Dottie reached out to accept the preacher's hand. Doing so, she felt as if a jolt of electricity had suddenly coursed through her body. "All of a sudden there was a feeling that I just can't describe," she declares. "It was a feeling of joy. I started crying and nothing was hurting me. It was just like I couldn't stop crying.

"And I was just happy. I was overjoyed. It was such an unusual feeling. It was like the Lord said: 'Okay, c'mon' . . . And something just tells you to move."

Her memories of what happened next are like snapshots in her mind, Dottie explains: There's a picture of her sister running up and also getting saved; another photograph of her grandmother shouting with joy and clapping her hands; yet another picture of the congregation shouting praises to the Lord; there's a snapshot of the preacher with a broad grin on his face.

As the years passed, Dottie continued to capture attention with her gift for music. One example took place when she was a freshman in high school, where there was a cardinal rule that no freshmen were allowed to sing with the older concert choir.

Dottie, of course, became the exception to that rule. "Well, I guess the teacher in the music department saw some special talent in me," she says, smiling. "I was the first freshman invited to sing in the choir."

High school became a showcase for Dottie's talents. "On Fridays, the students would participate in a local talent show," she relates. "Everybody would sing a song or something.

"And I would go to the piano and I could sing any song that was made by the Supremes, or Gladys Knight doin' 'The Midnight Train to Georgia.' I could mimic anybody, anything. And the kids just loved it and my choir director used to tell me all the time that I had talent."

At her high school graduation ceremony, the choir director made his feelings about Dottie's musical ability known to an auditorium filled with her teachers, friends, and family.

"He told everyone that he was sad because I wasn't going to go to college. But I was the oldest of ten kids, and I just wanted to get out of school and go to work and help my dad take care of the other kids. So that's what I did. I went to work to help the family out."

Her first job out of school was at the local hospital, she recollects. Dottie then accepted another job at General Motors so that she could be close to her father.

It was while she was still working at the GM factory that Dottie got her first major professional break.

"I was sixteen or seventeen when Dorothy Norwood came to Dayton," she recalls. "And she heard me sing at the church." To the teenager's surprise, the famed performer asked Dottie's mother if her daughter could tour with her for a while.

"My mom said yes, and I went on the road as a teenager with Dorothy Norwood for a year. And from that day to this day I've never done anything but stay in the music industry. With my singing, it was like God just said, 'Dorothy, this is where I want you to be.' "

Although she began to emerge in the musical forefront, it was at great personal cost, Dottie recalls. Instead of continuing with her gospel music career, she veered off the spiritual road and began singing pop and jazz.

"That was between being a teenager and a married adult," she recollects. "I sang jazz for a living because the money was real good and I was able to help support my family. And I was one of the baddest jazz singers you'd ever want to hear."

Although she was performing in nightclubs filled with almost every vice imaginable, Dottie asserts that she never fell prey to any of them.

"I never did any drinking, and I never smoked," she declares. "And I never got high. It's because my grandmother's teaching was still there inside me—her telling me to stay with the Lord."

Still, there was always a nagging voice in the back of her head that kept urging her to quit the nightclub scene. "I kept hearing that voice and it was always saying, 'You need to be back where you belong—in church.'"

Occasionally, that voice came from outside of her head. One of those times occurred when a friend of hers, Lincoln Berry, who played a church organ, sat Dottie down to have a talk with her. "I remember we were talking one day and he looked me in the eyes and he told me: 'Dottie, you need to be back where you belong.'"

It was a refrain she began to hear repeated over and over again from other people as well.

"I guess everybody perceived the spirit of the Lord in me," she submits. "I was well respected by my band, and all my promoters, and everybody always treated me with respect. But they all seemed to sense that deep-seated spirit inside me.

"They kept saying, 'C'mon, you don't need to be in them jazz clubs—you need to sing for the Lord.' But I was making very good money and helping to support my family."

Newly married, Dottie decided to move to Atlanta, Georgia, in order to be near her husband, who worked for Delta Airlines. Dottie recalls that her first order of business upon arriving in Atlanta was to find a church. She eventually settled on the Salem Baptist Church.

It was in that church where Dottie's life would take a complete turnabout. "I remember when I joined the church, they asked what auxiliary do you want to be in. And I said, 'The choir.'

"So I went to choir rehearsal that night. I was meeting my new best friend since arriving in Atlanta—Josephine—who was also a new member of the church. We both were interested in the choir. She had said, 'I'm gonna stay with you because I don't know nobody here.' So we went to the rehearsal together.

"When we got there, I told her, 'I'm gonna sit over there with the sopranos.' I sang soprano or alto. So we were sitting there and going over songs and stuff, singing a few little melodies. John Griggs, he was the choir director at the time, was teaching us parts."

What happened next still amazes the faith-driven gospel star. "I remember that I was sitting next to this woman—she didn't know me and I didn't know her—because I was a stranger in town. I had just joined the choir and nobody knew me.

"And all of a sudden she raises up her hand and she says to John, 'You need to give this girl right here—this new girl—a song. This girl got a *pretty* voice . . . and she can sing.' "

To this day the acclaimed gospel star remembers how startled she was by the woman's words. "I mean who was she to know that I was really wanting to sing in this choir—not in jazz clubs. I know she was a choir member, but I also was thinking that maybe she was an angel.

"I mean, here's a woman whom I don't even know—and I still can't even remember her name—and she just raises up her hand on my first night there and she says that they need to let me sing. It was like she was reading my mind."

Within moments, Dottie found herself being approached by the choir director. "He was saying to this woman, 'Let's see if this girl can sing.' And he said to me, 'Can you sing this song?' I said, 'Yes.' So John asked me to come down, in front of the choir, and to lead the song.

"And the first song I sang was 'Victory Shall Be Mine.' And at first the other choir members were mumbling about 'Who is this new girl?' You know how people go looking and mumbling. But then I started singing and the whole church was tore up—people started singing and clapping everywhere."

For the young singer, that moment nearly equaled the one when, at age ten, she felt God's presence. "The Lord started working on me," she testifies with a note of excitement in her voice. "He just started working on me.

"I had this sudden realization that this is what I wanted to do—I just wanted to sing for the Lord. I just wanted to see other people being healed through my singing.

"It worked on me to a point where I said to myself, 'This is what I'm gonna do. I'm never gonna sing jazz again.' And I never did sing jazz again. It was this angel—this lady whose name I can't even remember—who brought the Lord to me."

Suddenly, new opportunities began to present themselves, Dottie recalls. "The pastor recognized my talent and so we developed our own gospel label: Church Door Records. It was owned and operated by the Salem Baptist Church. And he made me general manager of it. I ran it and produced some records for it. I even recorded a couple of records."

Then Dottie met a record store owner who further advanced her career. "His name was Herb Lance and I made friends with him. He ran a record store in the city, Revelation Records, and he heard me sing because I had cut two records with Church Door. And he knew people at Atlanta International Records. That was a label that was distributed all over the country."

To her astonishment, Lance contacted the people he knew at the record company and urged them to audition the singer. "And he went and told them, 'You need to go over there and get that girl from behind the desk, 'cause she can really sing.'

"So my pastor said, 'I have no problem with her leaving, if that's what she wants to do.' And I signed with Atlanta International Records and I've been with them for six years now."

Dottie's first album for her new label, *Dottie Live,* did moderately well on the charts for the new artist. It was her follow-up record, *On Time God,* that established her as an industry icon.

By 1993, Dottie was on a steady course toward the stardom her great-grandmother had prophesied. That year, she won a Stellar Award nomination for Best Female Solo Performance—Traditional. In 1995, the vocal powerhouse won a record four honors at the Stellars for her album, *On Time God.*

The album also earned her the Atlanta Gospel Choice Award for Song of the Year. Dottie ended that whirlwind year by releasing a successful Christmas album, *Christmas With Dottie.* Other awards swiftly followed. In 1996, Dottie earned yet another Stellar Award as Female Vocalist of the Year.

"Everybody was coming to hear me sing, saying, 'Whoa, she's got so much talent she could be out there with Shirley Caesar or . . .' This was the dream I've always wanted. In my heart I always wanted to be a professional gospel singer. But I had to travel another road first."

Like the title to her award-winning album, the accomplished singer and songwriter believes that her life story proves that the Lord is an "on time God."

"When it was time he took me off that road," she declares. "God has His own way of doing things. He does things in His own time, when He wants to do it. When it was time He took me out of the jazz clubs and put me with Atlanta International Records. He did that and that's what you see in me today."

Although she is much appreciative of all the praise and awards that her talents have earned her over the years, Dottie modestly suggests that all the credit really belongs to the Almighty.

"God is getting the attention of those who don't know Him through my music," she attests. "I love singing, but it's my intimate relationship with the Lord—my desire to minister His Word and save souls—that inspires me to do it."

And she never forgets to thank the Lord for all his blessings. "When I'm traveling with my chorus [the People's Choice Chorale], when we hit the bus and we're all loaded on, the driver has to come from behind the wheel and join me and the musicians in prayer," she says.

"We join hands, and we pray and ask the Lord to send a traveling angel with us over the road. And in my private prayers I always ask the Lord to keep me humble. I never stop praying.

"People thought that when I recorded on a major label, and when I won the Stellars, that I was going to be different. But I haven't changed. Humility is the one thing that comes out of my mouth when I pray.

"No matter when I pray, I ask God to keep me humble. And I pray for my choir, for them to stay humble. And that has really worked for me, because I'm not an arrogant artist; I'm not a grand artist. God has made me stay right here. You know, no matter how high He takes me, I stay right here."

Dottie enjoys relating a story that illustrates just how important prayer is to her. "We were flying to a concert, and one of the singers was late," she recalls.

"I had all the tickets and was waiting for her. When she showed up and we got to the gate, all of the singers were gone—they had gotten on the plane. I looked at the attendant and I said: 'Could you please page People's Choice Chorale and have them get off the plane?'"

Dottie still chuckles at the airline attendant's reaction to her request. "And she said, 'Okay.' So, all of a sudden the stewardess makes this announcement: 'Will all the People's Choice Chorale please get off the plane.' "

Moments later, members of the ensemble began to disembark from the plane, expressions of confusion etched on their faces. "And they said, 'What happened? We get the wrong tickets or what?'

"They got off the plane and they were all standing out there, looking like: What's going on? And the stewardesses are also standing there, looking like: What's going on here?

"I said: 'You all know we don't travel anywhere without praying.' So we got out there in a circle, and we joined hands and prayed. *Then* we got on that plane. We don't do *anything* without praying."

The many blessings that God has bestowed upon her over the years are also available to anyone who seeks Him out, Dottie proclaims. "You've just got to keep God first in your life.

"I've kept Him first in my life and I don't take for granted what He's done for me—all the blessings He's bestowed upon me from the time I was in that church with my grandma."

Dottie adds it would also be a big mistake to take such blessings for granted—something she has never done.

"I appreciate that He has done all this for me, that He's made me part of the recent gospel explosion, and I'm reaching an audience that hasn't heard the Christian message before. Because He could bless somebody else and tell me to sit down.

"You've got to love Him and cherish Him and praise God for everything He's done for you and for all the blessings that He's bestowed upon you. You've got to remember that He could have blessed somebody else."

The gospel music star is also a firm believer in the benefits of tithing—giving back a percentage of one's earnings to some spiritual cause.

"That's what I tell everybody, even in my church when they call me up front to testify or to talk about my experiences on the road. I tell the audiences, 'You need to put Him first and give God back some of what He's given you. You need to tithe.' He blesses you more abundantly when you give back to Him.

"A lot of people don't realize that when you give to God, He gives you more. He just keeps blessing you more and more. That's worked for me. So if you want to be touched by God, don't forget to give back to God."

DONALD LAWRENCE

Photo by Russ Harrington

Donald is truly a remarkable young man. He's a man of many talents—especially musical talents. I predict that Donald will lead the gospel industry into the new century.

Not only does he write, arrange, produce, teach, and tour, but he also runs a business. I was amazed to learn that in addition to everything else going on in his life, Donald has a major administrative position in his recording company. In other words, he's in a decision-making position.

Donald is also a very disciplined individual. He has studied his craft, which I feel is essential for a solid and grounded gospel music entrepreneur. His wisdom will open doors for many who seek the high order in gospel music.

Above all, his belief in Christ is made obvious by his deeds. One does not necessarily always have to talk religion or Christianity to show allegiance. Action is the key sign of understanding. Donald exhibits Christian behavior constantly.

Donald Lawrence is another soldier who is touched by God.

$\mathcal{A}$s a result of having grown up a "lonely child," one of Donald's greatest personal struggles has been to control his overly sensitive nature. The Grammy-nominated and Stellar Award–winning performer relates that it often makes him feel vulnerable to both personal and professional criticism.

At such moments when the talented entertainer allows criticism to make him doubt his indisputable God-given talents, the Crystal Rose recording star relies on Scripture to center himself.

"The more popular you get, the more people pick and pull at you," asserts the North Carolina native, who has set the urban gospel market on fire with his electrifying Tri-City Singers ensemble. "And if you're a shy person who pretty much grew up alone like I did, it easily makes you want to go in and not come out."

But Donald maintains that there is also an upside to his sensitive nature: It has always made him feel as if he had a personal, one-on-one relationship with the Lord.

"Yeah, I definitely feel that," he asserts. "It's because of how I grew up. When you're lonely and shy, God becomes your best friend. So I've always felt that God was my special sidekick all through my life."

Born in Charlotte, North Carolina, and reared in the nearby Bible belt town of Gastonia, Donald's life got off to a bit of a rough start when, as an infant, he was turned over to his aunt and her best friend to be raised.

"My parents had gotten divorced, and even though I had brothers and sisters, I grew up like an only child," he relates. "I grew up with my mom's sister, my aunt, Ozella Brown."

When Ozella was at work, the youngster's care fell to one of his aunt's closest friends, Mamie Edwards, a woman who became a surrogate godmother to Donald.

"These ladies brought me to church as soon as I was old enough for them to carry me in there," he laughingly recalls. "I was probably one year old when I started going to church, and I've kind of been there ever since then.

"I loved church. If that's all you know, then you don't know how not to love it. My friends all went there, and I had some cousins that I used to hang around there with too. That's where I picked up music; that's where I learned everything!"

Donald still has fond memories of the Fire Baptized Holiness Church in Gastonia. It was there that, as a kid, the talented youngster sang in the choir, played organ and piano, and even started writing his own music at age sixteen.

"I always loved music," the versatile vocalist declares. "I wanted to make music and write plays. I remember my cousins' mom was very musical, and as little kids we all used to just sing. I was little but I was already learning about how to hear harmony and lots of things.

"So just by hanging around them and around church I picked up a lot about gospel music. And I used to watch their mother direct and teach the choir. Music became very much an interest of mine—it was a God-given gift."

Raised in a strictly religious household, music became Donald's main source of diversion.

"I never went to clubs and I never had an interest in going," he asserts. "I never experienced the alcohol scene or the drug scene at all. I never went through a swearing stage where I cursed or anything like that. I never did anything like that and I never missed it. I just grew up straight.

"I was very religious—and those were things you either did or did not do. I didn't do them. I'm not saying that I'm a Grade-A person for not doing any of those things. I'm just saying I had never done them and I didn't really miss not doing that kind of stuff."

Because he spent much of his time by himself, the accomplished singer remembers watching lots of television. "I used to always love the musicals on TV," he declares. "I was a young kid and I really didn't know what they were; I just knew that I enjoyed watching those people perform songs.

"I was one of those kids who, because I grew up by myself, I had a big imagination. I have this crazy memory bank," he says, chuckling. "I was able to remember everything off the musicals that I saw on TV: all the music, all the steps. All the little kids at church used to crack up at me because I remembered all the patterns.

"So I ended up in high school taking a drama class. It just all clicked for me because I could relate back to watching all that stuff on TV. And I started winning all these awards. My drama teacher talked to me and told me I really should consider musical theater."

Donald took his drama teacher's advice. Upon graduating from high school, he auditioned for and was accepted to the Cincinnati Conservatory, which the talented teenager attended on a scholarship.

But music wasn't enough for him. Donald resumed his pursuit of acting in addition to singing, writing, and playing musical instruments.

Graduating with a Bachelor of Fine Arts degree in musical theater, Donald recalls that his mind was set on Broadway.

"That was my whole dream," he declares. "I did a summer at the Burt Reynolds Dinner Theater in Florida, and after a few months that job came to an end. So I went home to decide what I wanted to do next."

Back home in Charlotte and without a job, Donald recalls that he and one of his friends decided to audition for evangelists Jim and Tammy Bakker's local PTL operation. "That was the time when Jim and Tammy were really heavy; it was like their heyday," he asserts.

"When they found out that I had a degree in musical theater, and I could direct shows, and I could choreograph and do all that stuff, they put me right to work. And it was great because in Charlotte, at that particular time, there was no place where you could work."

Donald worked for the Bakkers for about a year, taking full advantage of the opportunity to hone his various creative skills. "I was singing, I was producing—it was all like a Christian theme park, like Disneyland.

"I felt comfortable there because it was a place where you could really do gospel music and get a good salary for it. It was all done at a very good spiritual level. It was a really heavy-duty religious thing that the Bakkers were doing."

While working with the evangelists, one of the young entertainer's demos fell into the hands of Stephanie Mills, then a popular recording artist who had starred in the Broadway play *The Wiz*.

"A friend of mine had gotten one of my tapes to her, and she loved my work," he recalls. "So she just picked up the phone and called me, and asked me if I wanted to write some tunes for her. And I said, 'Well, I never wrote pop R&B tunes . . . but, you know, I can try.'

"And later on she called me back and said: 'I just lost my musical director, and I'd really love for you to come down and be my musical director on my tour."

Although it was an excellent opportunity for the ambitious young artist, Donald recollects that the decision to leave the PTL and work in the secular R&B industry was not an easy one for him to make.

"I wasn't really sure whether to do this. I'd led a strict church life and I was really uncomfortable with that kind of music. So I thought about it, and I finally decided to do it. And I ended up touring with her for ten years."

The accomplished artist makes no apologies for having spent nearly a decade in secular music. Donald is convinced that he was guided by God to do it.

"I was learning things. I was learning and using secular techniques that would later help me with my gospel music," he declares. "I was learning skills for producing. I was learning how to create live shows and how to create an album in the studio. It was definitely a classroom for me."

Donald also emphasizes that throughout those years he never really abandoned his involvement in gospel music.

"Even while I was doing Stephanie's stuff, I was still always doing my gospel stuff, 'cause that was me," he stresses. "You know, Stephanie's music was her music, but I still had my stuff. All of the criticism that I had 'moved to the other side' was bogus."

While working for the R&B singer, Donald not only managed to compose songs for the popular gospel group the Clark Sisters, but also found time to participate in the Gospel Music Workshop of America. Donald also wrote several gospel plays. One of those plays, *Sing Hallelujah!*, ran successfully at New York City's Village Gate for more than a year.

Then in his midtwenties, the versatile vocalist remembers deciding that "it was time for me to make my own statement." He notes that the decision to return to his gospel roots did not happen overnight; nor was it one of those moments when he heard God's voice suddenly encouraging him to do so. It simply was something that he had long wanted to do.

"I can't say there was any sudden transformation because I don't think I ever left gospel music," he submits. "It was just that I had been with Stephanie for almost ten years, and I always had all these gospel songs inside me.

"And now I really wanted to record them. It wasn't anything that I just prayed for and it suddenly came to me. These were songs that must have been birthed in me.

"So I decided to just take some money that I had saved up and do my own album. I got hold of a choir that was already established in the community, the Tri-City Singers; one of my friends was the director of it.

"And we developed a fresh sound 'cause I had come from that R&B thing, and it had a whole hip-hop flavor that gospel didn't have at that particular time. It was just something different. And I just did it and it kind of worked for me."

Donald began to organize his thirty-four-member urban-gospel-style ensemble in 1981. His mission, he recalls, was to put together a group that would "praise, raise, honor, magnify, and glorify the name of our Lord and Savior Jesus Christ."

Under his leadership, musical magic began to happen. The savvy musician began molding the Tri-City Singers "visually, philosophically, and stylistically" into one of the most colorful of contemporary gospel ensembles. "We turned it into a catalyst for what I consider the new sound in gospel now," he states. "We were something different."

With its funked-up, spiritual jams that blend up-to-the-minute urban music with old-fashioned choir vocals, Tri-City's 1993 debut album, *A Songwriter's Point of View*, went on to become an almost overnight success.

In 1995, the Tri-City Singers released *Bible Stories*. The record, with its foot-stomping interpretation of Bible stories, climbed effortlessly to the number two position on the gospel charts, and ultimately landed Donald and his choir on the list of the country's top ten gospel groups.

The Tri-City Singers rounded out that year with several Stellar Award nominations, as well as an NAACP Image Award nomination. In addition, the group received a Grammy nomination for the record and video.

"I can't take all the credit," Donald says with characteristic modesty. "I owe a lot of praise to Kevin Bond and everyone in Tri-City. And I thank God, who gave us the strength to make all these blessings happen."

The versatile vocalist also views his success as a reward from God for years of unswerving faith. "The Lord has always been with me," Donald declares with heartfelt emphasis.

"Faithfulness is definitely what God appreciates. He knows your heart, and He knows what you stand for and what you really want to do. And whenever you have that faithfulness, and when you have a close walk with Him, I think that's when He rewards you.

"If you're very faithful, you'll get what you're supposed to have. My reward was this gift for writing songs. It's probably my most extensive gift. I write songs that encourage people to come to Christ."

Like anyone who has received a gift, Donald is anxious to return one—which is why he is thinking about becoming an ordained minister. "I want to return His blessing with everything that I have at my disposal," he proclaims.

"I know that call is in my life right now. I just haven't announced that to everybody. So I really haven't made that complete step yet. But I'm definitely thinking about becoming a full-fledged minister. I actually plan to go to school for that."

What the Stellar Award–winning artist says he is waiting for is to make certain that God approves of his plan.

"I definitely want to walk with Him, but I really, really want to make sure that it's what He wants me to do," he asserts. "I want Him to know that I'm only doing this because I know He desires for me to do this. Because everything I do and say has to come from Him."

Although the popular performer remains one of the gospel music industry's prime examples of moral leadership, Donald candidly admits he is just as likely as anyone else to stumble and fall.

He acknowledges that one of his own biggest failures is sometimes doubting his own God-given talent whenever he feels "assaulted" by criticism.

"My faith is challenged that way even to this day," he

reveals. "You know, the more popular you get, the more people say things about you—you know, things you normally don't have to deal with. That kind of criticism makes you really wonder if you have something to offer. It makes you wonder if God has really given you something to say to people."

The faith-driven gospel star tries to view those moments of doubt as tests of his faith. "Yeah, it makes me sometimes feel like, 'Hey, let me forget all of this. I really don't need it and I really don't have to do it.' There've definitely been those times," he declares.

"And those times might have thrown me off a little bit. But, you know, eventually I bounce back. I'm a strong person. I just hold on to what I know He's given me. I just know that the talent He's given me is a pure thing and it's not counterfeit or anything. It's from my heart."

Donald adds that reading the Scriptures also helps to keep him centered. "I definitely think that the Scriptures can keep a balance in you. When I feel off balance they make me feel more comfortable and confident with myself, and then I feel more comfortable and confident with God."

Although his sensitive nature sometimes makes him feel like hiding out, Donald will not allow himself to do so. "I just love people really hard—even the ones who assault me," he laughingly declares. "And I try to really help everyone as much as I can."

He is particularly eager to reach out to teenagers—something that the artist already does a pretty good job of with his urban approach to gospel music. "I want participation from the kids," he asserts. "It's better to have them jammin' in church to my gospel music then hangin' on the streets."

Although Donald likes to describe himself as a "go-getter who wants to do it all," most of his future plans are limited to projects that will serve God. "There are so many things I want to do . . . but I also know that if I don't do them all I'm not going to die.

"When I go to sleep at night, I think about wanting to continually grow spiritually, because my spiritual growth is really the most important thing to me right now. Everything else is just like icing. Everything I do and say has got to come from Him."

For anyone desirous of a closer connection to God, Donald counsels that finding some serene moments for reflection is important. "All you need to do is get some quiet time," he advises. "You don't always have to be with people, even if you feel kinda lonely, or whatever.

"Get to know yourself, then you can get to know who God is. And you do that by getting into a quiet space. Just get alone, get away, and really learn who you are. Be confident in who you are."

He adds that once a person is comfortable with himself, it opens him to easier contact with God. "That kind of confidence brings you a lot of things, one of them being a closer walk with the Lord," he declares.

"And read the Bible. I definitely think that reading the Bible every day can keep you balanced. That's what I do! There's something about reading the Scriptures that will do more for you to get you closer to God than anything else, even if you don't understand them."

Donald adds that many of these sentiments were summed up in his song "In the Presence of the King." In it, he describes "what a privilege it is to be able to get into the presence of the King.

"When you develop a really strong relationship with Him and you become really good friends, He opens the door and lets you come into His presence where you can really sit before Him. He allows you to become a true worshipper."

And that's exactly what Donald wants to continue to do. "I feel that when you love Him, things work out the way they're supposed to work out," he declares. "Everything you want and desire will be granted if you bless Him and worship Him with everything you have."

VANESSA BELL ARMSTRONG

Photo by Gary Spector

Vanessa's voice has most frequently been compared to Aretha Franklin's. They say she has a young Aretha Franklin sound—and that's quite a compliment within the gospel field.

I've known Vanessa for many years, and I have always been very impressed by the wonderful way she uses her voice. It makes for a fabulous presentation.

This talented artist can sing anything, anytime, and anywhere. She's an absolutely superb performer. I look forward to seeing Vanessa continue to grow tremendously in the gospel music field, not only with her singing, but in her theatrical and other interests.

She's a fabulous artist in our industry—one who has been and I believe will continue to be touched by God.

For anyone wishing to gain an intimate glimpse into the soul of this inspiring artist, all that is really required is careful listening to the lyrics of some of her most popular songs.

In "Tears," Vanessa alludes to the emotional pain that she once suffered, and how with God's help she managed to get through those feelings.

In yet another song, "9th Month," the multi-Grammy- and Dove-nominated performer sings with truth-telling conviction about her "spiritual birth" after wanting to throw in the towel because of feelings of discouragement.

For Vanessa, who was "touched by God" in high school while singing a song in tribute to slain civil rights leader Dr. Martin Luther King, it all adds up to a lifetime of knowing what it feels like to be hurt, discouraged, or rejected. "I also know how it is to turn to prayer when you can't cry anymore," declares the Stellar Award–winning vocalist.

Although the Verity Records recording star says she is not yet ready to speak publicly about it, she doesn't disguise the fact that when she sings about the hurt she experienced in her life it has to do with an unhappy marriage.

What makes her hesitant to discuss the details is the effect it might have upon her children, as well as upon the ex-husband who since that time has mended his ways.

"The husband who caused me the unhappiness is not like that anymore," she emphasizes. "He's saved now, and I just don't want it to look like I'm trying to bash him . . . you know, to his kids. And another reason I don't want to talk about it is that I'm not sure how my kids would accept it."

But listen to her music and you will hear pieces of that story—in songs like "Tears," "Nobody But Jesus," and "Peace Be Strong." The Michigan native reveals that they all deal with memories of that painful episode in her life.

"Yeah, those songs came out of that," she acknowledges. "They came out of my longing for God to deliver me during that time."

Although the deliverance that she sought did arrive, Vanessa emphasizes that it did not take place overnight. The accomplished singer, however, does not fault the Lord for the delay, but only herself.

"It didn't happen until I really dealt with the issue and didn't use escapism," she declares. "Then He provided the deliverance I was seeking."

It's a lesson the twice-married singer and songwriter hopes other women in bad marriages learn from her. "Don't try to escape the pain you're feeling," she recommends. "Take an honest look at where you are and then turn it over to Him. Then He can provide for you."

Vanessa also promises that someday she will tell her whole story in a book, so that others can gain from her experience. "I'd like to be able to talk to women who have been through this," she states. "I'd like to tell them all about what I went through."

Despite such hardships, Vanessa has not become an embittered person. Instead, she continues to exude a joyful approach to life and demonstrates deep passion and concern for others.

That is why for more than a decade now, the gospel star has been utilizing her enormous God-given musical talents to lift people up and help deliver them from their problems.

"Every day in my life I try to help people," she proclaims. "I'm always lending a helping hand, whether it's financially, physically, or spiritually by talking to them. I'm always doing something, because it's not just in the church that I do this kind of work, but also outside of the church."

For this faith-driven performer, assisting others is a mission from God. It is fueled by a prophecy about her life in which she is supposed to be destined to enter the new millennium as a "musical messenger," helping people return to Jesus and inspiring upcoming gospel artists.

Vanessa relates that this prophecy was given her at a point in her life when she felt depressed about her career being over. "You know, everybody these days believes in psychics, crystal balls, and what have you," Vanessa offers.

"But there are people out there who are of God— they're ministers and missionaries of God, and God speaks through them. They're like the prophets of the Old Testament. And they told me about my going forth.

"I was getting older and feeling like my time was up. I just felt like it was time for me to just move on, because there were so many new artists coming up, with new things and what have you, and a new sound.

"I was saying, 'Well, hey, I've had my time. I've been out here now for over twenty years. But it wasn't just one prophet—it was several—and they all were saying to me, 'Oh, no, you may feel like you just want to give up, but your time is not through. You're getting ready to do a new thing; you're getting ready to go forth in this new generation. And you're getting ready to be an example.' "

Vanessa offers that she had been trying to set that kind of example long before she was made aware of the prophecy—beginning at the tender age of five when she first started singing in church.

"My mother always told me that I was born and groomed to sing the gospel and give my heart and soul," she declares.

Born the middle sibling of three girls who grew up on the Northwest side of Detroit, the gifted songstress fondly remembers that "we were like a big family on that street. I knew everyone and everybody knew me. Matter of fact, I sang for the kids on the block when I was only ten years old."

Vanessa has no memory of her neighborhood being a particularly tough one. "It was the kind of place where everybody looked out for everyone's children," she explains.

One of her favorite recollections is, as a youngster, showing off her vocal talents to an admiring audience of neighborhood kids.

"They would sit on my porch that had maybe seven steps, and they would line up on those steps each day," she laughingly recalls. "And I would stand out near the curb of the street. And it was like I was onstage, and I would sing."

Vanessa remembers one time when she misbehaved, and her mother punished her by canceling the talented youngster's daily musical performance. "I figured out a way to beat her," Vanessa says, smiling.

"I thought about it and I figured out a way to sing even though I was being punished. I just stood inside of the screen door and belted out my songs. The kids came, anyway."

Vanessa has always possessed that kind of determined and outgoing personality, even as a little girl. "I was a very, very bold, outspoken girl. I liked to sing, and I was very outstanding at that.

"And every time we'd go to choir rehearsal, and they would ask who would lead the song, I would be the main one. I remember the choir director once said to me, 'You can't lead 'em *all*, Vanessa.' So I wasn't shy at all. I was very, very bold."

It was the music more than the preaching at Detroit's North End Church of God in Christ that always attracted her, she recalls. "My daddy—he was also a good singer—would always say that I either talked or slept through the rest of the service.

"But when I heard my name called to sing, then I would jump up and go up there and sing. So, I basically went for the singing, until the preaching, the Word, got to me."

Reminiscing about her parents, Vanessa recalls that Mildred and Jesse were "just regular people. My father worked in a Chevrolet plant for almost all of his life, until he retired and became a minister. He always talked about becoming a minister and then the Lord called him.

"And my mother was a housewife. She went to church, and she kept us groomed, and kept us going to church. It was just the basic, average family."

Dinner was a special time reserved for religious discussion. "My daddy always had the Bible open," she recalls. She adds that religion was an important part of family life during other times of the week as well. "We had to go to church; it was mandatory. We *had* to go before we could do anything else."

Although Vanessa enjoyed religion, as a teenager she remembers staging a brief rebellion against it. It stemmed, she explains, from her mother's repeated insistence that she follow in her father's footsteps and become a minister.

"My mother just kept telling me about the dream that she once had—that we were in a dark pit. Me and my mother were in a real dark pit. And my father was standing in a bright light.

"And in this dream she asked the Lord how we could come out of this pit. And He said to my mother: 'Promise me the little one will follow in her father's footsteps.' And when she said, 'Yes, Lord,' we came out of the pit, and we were standing with my father."

As a child, Vanessa remembers being profoundly affected by the telling of that dream. By her teenage years, however, it began to wear on her. "You know, it was cute when I was little, because, you know, it was true. I was a little girl and I was able to sing just like my daddy. I mean, at the age of five I was already singing. And it was just fantastic.

"But, then, as I got older, I started thinking about that call on my life. I started figuring out, well, why was everybody else getting a chance to make a choice of what they wanted to do? Why was mine already chosen?

"I started wanting to sing a little secular music—I wanted to be like Aretha Franklin. And so every talent show I went to, I would get up there and sing one of Aretha's songs.

"I just wanted to see what was on the other side, and it was probably because my mother kept saying I couldn't, couldn't, couldn't. Don't, don't, don't. And that just became more tempting for me to see what was out there."

Vanessa recalls that each Sunday she would be saved in church, but come the rest of the week she was doing her own thing, which was mostly singing the R&B songs of her favorite artists.

"I just loved Aretha. I loved Gladys Knight, all of the artists. And I just wanted to sing a little bit of that. That's all I used to do, and it really wasn't very much."

Vanessa remembers that any time she decided to succumb to some other temptation, it was always short-lived because she felt guilty and uncomfortable doing so.

"I didn't drink, I didn't do drugs, I didn't party," she submits. "I once tried to smoke a cigarette and I almost coughed myself to death." She laughs. "I tried to go to a club, and I looked like a wallflower.

"I tried to act like I was gonna be drinking, but I couldn't stand alcohol. It just wasn't me. I remember I was at that club and a person came up to me and said, 'Well, why don't you go home? You look out of place.' So I never did that anymore."

Although Vanessa continued to attend church throughout this rebellious period, there was one special moment when the teenager was suddenly so overwhelmed by God's spirit that all her contrary behavior suddenly ceased.

That spiritual moment took place immediately following the assassination of the civil rights leader, Dr. Martin Luther King, while Vanessa was in school singing a song in tribute to the slain black leader.

"I sang 'Precious Lord' in the school auditorium after Martin Luther King passed, and that's when all my running from God ceased," she declares. "It was like I felt the Lord speaking to me, saying, 'You know, this is what I want you to sing.'

"That's when I started giving my heart and soul to the Lord. An overwhelming sensation came over me when I was singing that song. It was like warmth."

Recalling that moment, the accomplished gospel artist remembers looking out at the faces before her and watching them dissolve into tears. "I figured they were crying because of Martin Luther King," she asserts. "I didn't realize that they were crying because of my singing."

"Maybe it was the song that was touching them at the appropriate moment. But I know I was crying, because the Lord spoke to me while I was singing it and I just—I had never experienced that before."

Walking off that stage, Vanessa felt herself spiritually renewed. "I just knew what I was supposed to do," she offers. "I didn't act any differently, I just knew what my charge was. I knew what my fulfillment of life was supposed to be, and what He put me on this earth to do. It was to sing the gospel and be a minister of songs."

When she returned home to tell her parents what had transpired, they reacted joyfully. "They were so happy," she recollects. "My mother felt that her dream was finally fulfilled.

"She always knew, even though I was trying to do other things, that I wouldn't go too far. 'Cause they were praying people—they still are—and they were always praying for me."

While still in her teens, the talented youngster with the soul-filled vocal power soon moved on from singing in the North End Church of God in Christ choir to traveling the gospel circuit and performing on shows with luminaries such as Rev. James Cleveland, the Clark Sisters, the Mighty Clouds of Joy, and the Winans.

It was while she was performing at one of the late Reverend's workshops in 1984 that Vanessa, at the time married to her first husband, experienced an important turning point in her career.

She was discovered by a talent scout from Benson Records, who offered the young singer a recording contract. Vanessa went on to record three best-selling albums for that label.

The award-winning gospel artist gained even more recognition in 1987 when millions of viewers became familiar with her voice as the singer of the theme song for the popular NBC sitcom *Amen.*

That same year, Vanessa's popularity increased another notch when the versatile artist made her mark on Broadway with the hit musical *Don't Get God Started,* then touring nationally with the play and winning audiences over with her vocal gymnastics.

Other accomplishments quickly followed, including nominations for both the Grammy and Dove awards, and an appearance in the television movie *The Women of Brewster Place,* with Oprah Winfrey.

Although Vanessa has been inspiring, uplifting, and delivering God's message to audiences everywhere for just over a decade now, the premier performer has not forgotten the discouraging times when her faith was challenged.

"There were times—you know, there've been several times—that I've asked God why? It seemed like my path wasn't going smoothly, and I just figured, 'If it can't get no better than this, what's the purpose?' "

Vanessa is reticent to offer any further details, other than to say that in addition to the problems her marriage was suffering, there was a time when, deeply discouraged about the pace of her professional career, she was ready to throw in the towel.

"It's too personal for me to talk about," she declares. "But I can tell you that I was in my twenties, and I already had a couple of children. I was feeling depressed. It was a time when I questioned the future of my career."

That low point in her life was another time when the acclaimed singer believes she was touched by God. "He started to speak to me. He started coming to me through the Scriptures," she recollects.

"I would always just pick up the Word, and He would give me the Scripture that would answer my concerns. It was like He was just talking to me. Or I'd hear the Word in church, and it seemed like the preacher was just preaching right to me. It really got me through that period."

Vanessa believes all the blessings that she has received from the Lord over the years simply bear out the words of the prophecies that were once given her.

"I just think I was chosen," she asserts. "You know, they say many are called, but few are chosen. I was chosen to do this kind of work, and so He has had His hand on me. It was predestined for me to walk with Him.

"And I don't care what I do, or what I say, or how I try to get away from Him, I know that I've been chosen by God. There's no way me getting around it, unless I totally walk away from Him. But as long as I know what my life is supposed to be like, and I believe in Him, He will always direct my path."

Vanessa doesn't believe she holds any kind of exclusive contract when it comes to God's blessings.

"Just seek Him more," she counsels. "The more you seek Him, the more He'll open Himself to you. He will come closer to you. And you'll feel that closeness, and you'll feel that unity—that oneness that He's there, all the time. And He'll help you."

For anyone suffering from feelings of discouragement, Vanessa further advises that they not give up hope as she once nearly did. She also suggests honest self-examination.

"Just turn it over to Him. I've realized that whatever state you're in—I know that when I've gotten into situations—I had to really look at it and see why I was there.

"Was it because I did it, or was it because it was just meant for me to be in that particular position at that moment? And if it wasn't anything that I did, then I figure that's where God wanted me to be at that particular moment—until He moved me further on. Every trial is for a reason."

Speaking from her own personal experience, the accomplished singer believes that even negative situations can make a person stronger. "Everything that I've been through in my life, I've found has made me stronger—and I've been through a whole lot," she declares.

"I've been through two marriages, and I have six kids. And I often wonder: How in the world did I make it? And why did I go through some of the things that I went through? It was to make me stronger. And I now know that I'm a strong woman in Christ."

Vanessa is a big believer in prayer, especially in times of trouble. Even when things are going well for her, prayer is very much part of her everyday life.

"At certain times, when I really feel the need to dedicate myself to God, I will assign times to pray—me and a prayer partner. It's usually in the mornings, 'round five-thirty or six in the morning.

"And then before I go to bed at night I pray. But all day there's a prayer in my spirit, because I realize that you don't know what's gonna happen each second. So I constantly pray.

"I pray, 'Lord, direct me, and tell me what to do.' Because I'm out here . . . this is the real world. I always have obstacles, challenges, things coming my way. If it's not my teenage kids, it's just always something that comes to kind of knock me offtrack and to challenge me."

Vanessa says she anticipates the years to come with enthusiasm—especially her prophesied role for the new millennium.

"I no longer believe that I'm at the end of my career, that I've reached a certain level and that's it," she declares. "But I have this burning for God in my heart and soul and I'm ready to go. I'm ready to go forth in this new generation and to help more people receive the gospel. I'm getting ready to be the example."

And Vanessa asserts she is not going to limit the forums she uses—including television and movies—to spread God's word. "I've not even touched the surface of where I'm getting ready to go," she proclaims.

The gospel great adds that she is not concerned about criticism, because she has already dealt with that issue. A shade of annoyance comes into Vanessa's voice when the gospel star recalls how she was attacked for performing the *Amen* theme song.

"I told those people who criticized me, 'You've followed me all these years. You know what I stand for, so you don't even have to question what I am singing about.' I told people, 'You know me better than that.' And that nipped that right in the bud."

What is most important to her is that she only use her unique God-given musical gift to showcase her love for the Lord.

"I just keep in mind my motive. I just remember what I've been charged to do from God. As long as you've got that burning in your heart and soul, you can't go wrong."

DARYL COLEY

Photo by Reisig & Taylor

There are voices and then there are exceptional voices. Daryl has an exceptional voice and is loved and admired by many in this industry. When I think of Daryl, I feel respect. He is an extraordinary soldier in the gospel army. His rich background as a jazz singer and background singer for many world-renowned artists puts him in a position of mastery.

Daryl's lovely wife and two children, whom I know personally, represent a support base and stability worthy of notice. When Daryl shared his experience with me about his lifestyle on the streets that he broke away from as a teenager, I was somewhat stunned and pleased to witness his declaration of deliverance. He has a wonderful testimony.

Daryl was the first gospel artist to record an album project on my weekly television *Gospel Explosion* show. I was truly excited that he had that much respect for us to want to record an album at our affair.

But more than all that, Daryl is a man with a heart and a true knowledge of the Lord. His story will truly inspire and encourage you. Daryl is very much touched by God.

There were two occasions in his life when the singer, songwriter, and pastor cried out to the Lord for assistance. The multi-Grammy-nominated performer remembers that in both instances, God responded to his heartfelt pleas—not overnight, but as a "process."

The first occurrence took place when the prominent praise singer was a teenager. Daryl had become weary of his fast-paced lifestyle of "alcohol, drugs, and struggles with the flesh." But he felt unable to shake free of his attraction to that kind of life without God's help.

Years later, the talented singer and songwriter again reached out for God's hand, this time to cope with the brutal murder of his manager and best friend. That loss plunged him into a tailspin of despair from which the award-winning performer thought he would never emerge.

The forty-three-year-old California native, who in his distinctive musical career has recorded more than seven albums for Sparrow Records and once performed at the White House, today regards both those events as major spiritual milestones in his life.

"I didn't become more religious, because religion is man's search for God," the Dove and Stellar Award–

winning gospel star proclaims. "But it made me more relationship-oriented with Jesus. Establishing a relationship is real intimacy. Instead of understanding Him from an intellectual level, I began to understand Him with my heart as well."

Reared in a devoutly Christian home in the East Oakland area of San Francisco, Daryl recalls that his religious instruction began at an early age. His father, an aircraft engineer, served as one of the teachers at the local Sunday school, while his mother, a secretary at the nearby Alameda Naval Air Station, was choir director at her church.

Daryl suggests that because religion was of such importance to his family, the nearby Mount Zion Baptist Church, which he and members of his family frequently attended, became almost like a second home for him.

"I was always in that church until I was about twelve, at least on Saturday and Sunday," he recollects. "Saturday night was studying for Sunday school, Sunday was church.

"And church was a family affair—the whole family was there. My father went there, my great-aunt, and my godmother. My godfather visited occasionally and my godmother's mother was a mother of the church. So it was like a family environment."

Perhaps the only member of the family who did not attend that Baptist church was Daryl's mother, who worshipped at Oakland's Ephesians Church of God, which the youngster began attending at age twelve.

Daryl remembers it was more than just the Word that was instilled in him as a youngster. There were many lessons that focused upon morality, as well.

"My mom and dad would always be talking to me about right and wrong attitudes," he relates. "There wasn't a whole lot of talk about religion. I think religion was left up to my discretion and determination because they came from different denominations. We would mostly talk about good morals and good common sense."

Besides his solidly rooted biblical beginnings, Daryl was also grounded in music. His mother was a talented gospel singer herself, and served as an early inspiration for her musically gifted son.

Daryl still fondly recollects how his mother always encouraged him to further develop his musical talents—which he did with gusto. "It was pretty much my mom who got me on the gospel pathway," he maintains.

By the time he was in grade school, Daryl was not only playing clarinet in the school band, but was also taking voice and jazz piano lessons. At age seven, the musically blessed youngster was a featured vocalist in his home church, as well as the citywide Oakland Children's Chorus.

The eldest of three siblings, Daryl recalls the neighborhood he grew up in as a "quiet black community, a middle-class kind of place."

He describes himself as having been a "relatively quiet kind of kid—but maybe you should ask my mother about that," he adds, smiling. "I wasn't rowdy or anything because in our house we were taught good morals."

Although religion was part and parcel of his life—and he enjoyed it—in church it was the praise music that mostly interested him. "I was always intrigued by the music," he recollects. "I mean, it was always something I looked forward to."

There was other music that filled his life as well. Although his household was a devoutly Christian one where gospel music would always be playing on his parents' Victrola, Daryl was not discouraged from listening to other forms of music as well. Jazz, classical music, and R&B were as much part of the future gospel star's musical environment as gospel. Still, Daryl remembers always having a special affection for spiritual music.

"Although I listened to and sang everything else, I was always singing the church songs," he explains. "Church songs were always the stuff that came up before anything else did."

After joining Oakland's Ephesians Church of God, a whole new dimension of gospel music began to open to the talented youngster. It was that church where future gospel luminaries Edwin and Walter Hawkins, then still teenagers, were cutting their musical teeth.

Within a year, the Edwin Hawkins Singers' "Oh Happy Day" had catapulted them to the top of both the gospel and pop charts, and the wide-eyed youngster watched as what was once music only sung in church caught on fire in the secular music industry. It gave Daryl much to think about in the years to come.

Daryl sadly recalls that his spiritual life took a downturn during his teenage years. It was then that the acclaimed performer succumbed to the temptations of East Oakland's fast street life, unable to resist the alcohol, drugs, and easy sex.

"I never really left the church, but I think everybody has a tendency to test the waters, especially teenagers," he thoughtfully reflects. "So I dealt with drugs and alcohol—you know, it was peer pressure—and sexual experimentation. That kind of stuff."

Daryl offers that he became absorbed with that kind of life from junior high school through his high school years. But although he was acting out in ways that were quite contrary to his religious upbringing, he remembers never quite feeling comfortable with his lifestyle.

"If you train a child in the Word, then that child won't ever really depart from the Word," he submits. "So even though I was doing those other things, the Word of God was staring me in the face and it drew me back to a relationship with the Lord."

The accomplished singer emphasizes that his return to God was not an overnight experience. Instead, it was what Daryl likes to describe as a "process."

He goes on to explain his use of that word: "I think every person should understand that from the point when they begin to believe—believe totally in the Lord—they start to go through a process. It's a step-by-step, line-by-line, precept-by-precept process.

"They begin to move toward becoming more like Him, more Christ-like in their attitude and in their lifestyle. It's not an immediate, all-of-a-sudden kind of thing—a wondrous change.

"It's a process of changing. And then you find yourself in situations and doing things that used to affect you, but no longer have an effect on you. The things you do, or used to do, you don't have an appetite for anymore and don't even consider doing them."

Which is how the Lord began operating on him, Daryl explains.

"I was coming to the end of myself," he recollects. "I was getting tired of the circle that I was involved in. I found myself repeating stuff that I'd been through and wondering, 'How come I'm not getting out of this?'

"You know, some people never wake up. But there are others who wake up and say, 'Hey, wait a minute . . . I've done this, you know, two or three times. I don't want to repeat this again. There's gotta be something better, something different, something more real than what I'm dealing with.' "

Although changes were beginning to take place, Daryl was eager to begin his new life. Realizing that he lacked the strength to speed up the process, the teenager turned to the Lord for help.

"I remember feeling, 'Hey, I'm at the end of this thing. I'm tired of it, I'm tired of myself. I'm tired of the condition, the situation. Things are not changing—so, God, please help me.'

"You know, if I could've changed things in my life, then I would already have done so. But seeing as these things were beyond my control, I turned to the power of God. I knew His power was greater than my own. And I began to cry out and seek Him. I asked the Lord to begin to change my life, and He began doing it."

As a start, Daryl began to read the Scriptures. "I read the Word and tried to find out what it said about where I've been, and what I'd been doing. It was part of the process of becoming a new person, and it worked!

"It was the conviction of the Word that drew me back," he attests. "I just began to seek Him out. I think it just happened because it was predestined for it to happen. It was predestined for me to have a relationship with Jesus Christ.

"And when you begin to seek Him, then the things that are of the flesh, the things that are of the world, begin to fade and aren't effective in your old way of life. Now you're totally seeking the things of God, and the mind of God, and the heartbeat of God.

"And the more you find out about Him, the more blessings He gives you. That whetted my appetite for more revelations from Him. All I wanted to do was please Him. So I continued to seek."

Although the acclaimed gospel star honestly admits there were still some moments when he slipped off the path, he remembers that, for the most part, his spiritual stride became steadier and steadier.

"You know, even after begging for God's help, I went to parties and drank to get drunk," he relates. "I remember drinking as much alcohol as I used to. But I couldn't get drunk. I didn't get a buzz or anything from it. And that meant, from that point on, I didn't need to have alcohol.

"I said, 'Hey, it's not effective for me.' I mean, God took the cry of my spirit and my heart and said, 'Hey, you made a covenant with me, and I'm gonna keep my end of the bargain.' And He did exactly that!"

Daryl, who does not come off as a person who enjoys a great deal of emotional hullabaloo, describes his conversations with God in quiet terms.

"You know, a lot of people testify that when they heard God's voice the Lord said, 'Don't, don't, don't.' But it wasn't like that for me; it wasn't that kind of thing."

"Yeah, his voice was audible—it's always audible to those who have an ear to hear it—but it was more like the Lord just challenged me. His challenge unto me was: 'If you're gonna become more like me, then the things that you are have to die, so that I can begin to live in those places that used to be you.'

"And what that said to me was that as I continued to walk and seek Him, I had to become more like Him. That I was also responsible for being a representative of Him. And some of the things I was doing were not the right representation of a Kingdom of God person."

It was a comforting message, Daryl recollects. "I came to realize how gracious and merciful He was for forgiving me. I also realized how you can still make mistakes—have flaws, even after you've made a covenant with Him.

"But I also understood that there's the perfect gift of God even in an imperfect vessel like myself who was on his way to perfection. That's why there's grace and mercy."

For Daryl, the struggles he underwent with his conscience were not something new to him. The thoughtful and intelligent singer and minister recalls that even as a youngster he had earned a special nickname from his friends—"preacher"—because of his high moral values.

"The kids used to always call me preacher," he says, smiling. "Even through elementary school. I mean, the mark of the Lord was on my life without any effort of my own. It was already there: preordained, predestined by God.

"Even back then, when kids are kids and do stuff that kids do, there was stuff I wouldn't participate in. I wasn't a tattletale, but I just wouldn't participate.

"Or I'd tell 'em, 'Hey, that ain't the right attitude to have.' 'Cause, again, even as a young kid, I was going to Sunday school, going to church, and my mom had told me definite things about right and wrong attitudes."

Today, reflecting upon his life on the streets and the changes he underwent, Daryl describes it as his "Damascus Road experience. It's where the Lord knocked me down, knocked me out for a little while.

"And then he began to minister to me and give revelation. And when He gave me 'back my spiritual sight,' then I was like Saul, whose name was changed to Paul." Daryl, wearing his pastor's hat, enjoys making a comparison between Paul's change of heart and his own. "I had good religion and, you know, Saul had good religion. I was faithful to choir rehearsal, and I studied my Sunday school lessons, and so forth. And I paid my tithes and I was baptized at thirteen. But I still had fleshly desires. Because even though I was reading the Word, and so forth, there was not an *understanding*—not a revelation—of what the Word was actually saying. That didn't happen until I got to the place of trying not so much to understand it with my head, but to listen to Him with my spirit and my heart."

While Daryl was busily engaged in shedding his old skin, he relates that he did not forgo his love of music. In high school, the teenager sang with a vocal ensemble called the Castleers, performing everything from classical numbers and show tunes to pop, R&B, and jazz. He also took music classes with such future luminaries as Freddie Washington and keyboardist Rodney Franklin.

When fellow Castleer Franklin landed a record deal with Columbia Records soon after graduating from high school, the newly signed artist called on his old school buddy to help him with the background and vocal arrangements on his album.

It was during these sessions that Daryl became friendly with Franklin's producer, celebrated jazz artist Stanley

Clarke. Clarke was to become instrumental in getting the talented young musician his first major break in show business.

"Stanley called me late one night and said, 'Daryl, I've got to do this album with Ramsey Lewis and Nancy Wilson, and the thing is set up for tomorrow. Can you come and do it?' "

Excited at the opportunity, the young musician eagerly agreed. The result of that recording session was the record's title duet, a smash hit called "Just the Two of Us," in which Daryl performed with the two popular jazz and R&B artists.

Although by 1977 Daryl was poised as one of the most promising upcoming artists in the world of secular jazz, the accomplished musician remembers that deep in his heart he had never stopped loving the less glitzy but spiritually satisfying gospel music he had been reared with.

So Daryl began to split his time between working with jazz and R&B artists and participating in the gospel arena as well.

He also participated in the Edwin Hawkins Music and Arts Seminar, a training ground for many of today's top gospel music stars, and attended the late Rev. James Cleveland's Gospel Music Workshop of America. In addition, the talented singer and songwriter performed as a member of a popular local gospel group, the Voices of Christ.

"It was something I was always carrying around in my mind," he asserts. "I just always wanted to go back to my roots and these were some of the ways I was doing it. It just felt right for me."

In 1983, after writing the title song for Tramaine Hawkins's smash hit album, *I Am Determined,* Daryl began to tour with the popular gospel artist as keyboardist and musical director.

Later, the versatile performer moved to Los Angeles to work as a soloist with James Cleveland's organization. In

1985 Daryl released his first of seven solo albums, *Just Daryl*, on a small label called Plumline Records.

The album earned him a Grammy Award nomination and four GMWA Excellence Awards, including Best Artist, Best Album, Best Male Vocalist, and Best Song.

Music critics could not give enough praise to the talented newcomer, who was described by one writer as "forging a distinctive sound that mates the lush gospel-chorale style with sophisticated musical arrangements that wouldn't be out of place on an Anita Baker record."

All the pieces were finally coming into place for the youngster from the streets of Oakland, when tragedy struck. It was an event that nearly put an end to his promising career.

Even today in relating that story there is a note of pain in his voice. "I had a manager from Detroit at one time," he begins, adding that he would prefer not to mention his friend's name. "I became very close with him. We were like brothers. I lived in California, but I had a key to his place and even his car key. If I was coming through town, I had access to everything he had. And we set up a few things, we were mapping out some things."

Then in his thirties, Daryl was exuberant over his recent successful tour with Tramaine Hawkins. Meanwhile, his first solo album was selling briskly.

Daryl was convinced that he was on the verge of a breakthrough in his career. And he gave much credit for that to his friend and manager. Then the person Daryl depended upon so much was discovered brutally murdered.

"The police never really found out what happened," Daryl relates. "I became very upset, because it seemed like everything was in line to go right. I said, 'Wow, some great doors are opening up for me; some things that I'd like to do are beginning to come through.'

"It was through this friendship that I had this business relationship. But all of that came to an end when he was murdered. So when I got the news that they had found him dead, it was devastating to me. I went into a deep depression."

Daryl remembers learning of his friend's death just as he was getting ready to step into the recording studio to cut a new record in Atlanta, Georgia. "They told me all this just a couple of hours before I was supposed to be in the studio," he recollects.

Badly shaken by the news, the very next morning the distraught singer headed to the nearest bar in order to drown his sorrows. It was a habit Daryl thought he had left behind him as a result of his new covenant with the Lord.

"I had about four or five Long Island Iced Teas," he recollects. "I was just trying to numb the pain and all that kind of stuff. His death wrecked me so, some friends came and got me out of there and kept me in their homes for a couple of days. They just kind of watched me because it was so devastating to me."

Daryl recalls that the sadness and pain he felt was so overwhelming, that he gave serious consideration to quitting the music business altogether. "I was saying to anyone who'd listen that I was through with it. It was a period that I went through for two or three months.

"I remember I was saying that I didn't want to sing, I didn't want to preach, I didn't want to play music—I didn't want to do nothing. I just wanted to be alone. And I felt angry at the Lord. I said, 'If this is the way you're gonna do things, and this is the way you're gonna treat me . . .' "

Today, Daryl can only smile at the memory of that temper tantrum. "And, you know, He let me have my tantrum. He let me have my little pity party for a while, and then He began to minister to me. He began to minister unto me, and began to heal me emotionally from that point on."

Almost mysteriously, people began showing up in his life to comfort him, he recalls. Some of the faces Daryl recognized, while others were complete strangers to him.

"The Lord began to send people to pray for me," he testifies. "They were prayer warriors. They would come and just take my hand, and just really pray for me."

Still bitter about the loss he had suffered, Daryl recollects how reluctant he was initially to accept the solace and support that was being offered him.

"At first, I accepted their prayers but I had this attitude, you know, 'Yeah, go ahead and pray if it's going to make you feel better.' But they ignored that tone in my voice and they ministered to me."

It was then that Daryl witnessed another miraculous event, one that to this very day he has never forgotten. "The Lord began to visit me in my dreams," he proclaims with a note of awe in his voice. "He began to show me, or teach me, how to trust Him and rely on Him."

It was in one of those dreams, Daryl recollects, that God gently counseled him that he did not need to rely on a manager in order to become successful—only upon the Lord. It was a message that Daryl says he has never forgotten.

"I learned not to put confidence in or trust the flesh, because people always have good intentions, but sometimes circumstances, situations—and even their own failings—cause them not to be able to do what they intended to do. And that sets up a major disappointment.

"So the Lord began to teach me to trust Him and rely on Him, even though people made promises. That's why, even today, I don't get excited about what people promise to do for me. I just wait and see if it comes to pass. And the things that God says always come to pass."

Between the constant appearances of the prayer warriors and his God-filled dreams, Daryl's fallen spirits gradually began to rise. "That's literally how God began to lift me," he proclaims. "It came to a point where the pain I was feeling was beginning to disappear.

"Even though there was a temporary 'no' in me, a turning my back on the Lord, there always is an eternal 'yes' unto the Lord. And from that place of the eternal 'yes,' He began to work through my temporary 'no.' And I began to be healed."

There is another important lesson that the gospel great learned from his ordeal: that there was no harm or shame in expressing anger toward the Almighty. "God wasn't challenged by my anger," he offers.

"It was a true emotion and He already knew it was there. It's not like they teach you in church, that you're not supposed to question God and ask why, that you're never supposed to say you're angry with God."

Daryl, who is today the pastor of his own California church, submits that he often emphasizes that point from the pulpit.

"He would prefer that we recognize our anger and direct it toward Him rather than keep it concealed or shy away from it . . . or put on a facade for everybody else to see," he declares.

"He can handle that anger. He can speak to us out of that anger—because it's an open place—and begin to heal us. What I had to do was put the anger I was feeling on the table before God and really deal with it. He and I had to deal with it. And when I opened that up to Him, that's when He began to heal me emotionally."

As his healing continued, Daryl recalls beginning to feel eager to get back to work. No longer was his soul divided between whether he should continue to play secular or gospel music. The choice now had become a clear one for him.

"I didn't jump right back into it," he explains. "It was a process and it happened slowly. I began to feel that He wanted me to perform my music. He was restoring my love for gospel music. My soul searching was over."

Today, as a result of his own hurtful experience, the singer/songwriter/preacher feels he is qualified to counsel those who are going through some hardship.

"If you're in pain or angry, the first place you start is on your knees," he advises. "Don't get on the phone counseling with anybody. Don't pick up the Bible and try to read it, because your pain or your anger won't let you understand or hear or see revelations—your pain will not allow you to receive healing.

"So get on your face; you don't even have to get on your knees. Cut the TV off, cut the telephone off, cut the music off. If you're in your car, park it and scream.

"If you gotta walk, walk around your house and just holler and cry, but get it out! Talk to God. You know, audibly. Talk to Him and leave a place after you vent your emotions. Leave a place for God to speak back to you—and expect it."

The venting of pent-up feelings is vital in order to capture God's ear, Daryl asserts. He stresses that the cry to the Lord for help must be a deeply emotional and honest one, accompanied by a release of any pent-up anger either toward God or oneself.

"It's the cry, 'Hey, I'm at the end of this thing. I'm tired of it. I'm tired of myself. I'm tired of the condition and the situation.' And when you get to that point, then you turn to the power of God, which is greater than you. And you ask the Lord to begin to change your life. And He does it."

Next, Daryl counsels that it is important just to "sit still and listen" for God's voice. "Get it all out of your system, but begin to listen. Just remember that this is temporary, what you're going through. God already knows about what you're going through. Nothing happens by surprise to God—it's all by design."

As a final step, the faith-driven artist recommends seeking out qualified Christian counseling. "Get hold of those you know who have the ear of God, and just ask them to pray for you. If they have the ear of God, when they pray the Holy Spirit will give them what they need to help heal you."

The veteran performer also contends that for people uneasy about baring their souls to strangers, it is not really necessary to do so. "Just tell them, 'Pray for me.' If they really know God, they'll just do that automatically, anyway."

In his own life, prayer plays an important role, Daryl asserts. He does much of it both at his Los Angeles–based Love Fellowship Tabernacle Church and at home.

The gospel star reveals that he usually arises at four-thirty in the morning for prayer. "It's real quiet in the house and I take that time to just meditate upon the Lord, and worship Him, and bless Him, and to listen.

"My prayers usually deal with clarity, and with understanding. I try to understand what His will is. And I also bless Him and ask Him to continue to provide for my family, that kind of thing.

"I guess my prayers are just to make sure that I'm in the center of His will, and that He is pleased with what I'm doing. You know, I've gone past trying to please people, 'cause they're fickle. They like one thing this week and something else next week. So I don't have to deal with that. If I please God, I know that all things are in order."

Looking toward the future, the versatile vocalist, who has been married for more than seventeen years and is the father of three children, sees himself taking on more ministerial duties. He is already working toward that goal, trying to raise funds to construct a new, larger church building.

The acclaimed musician says he is certain about one thing in the years to come: He will remain committed to gospel music. Daryl goes on to explain that to this very day secular record labels try to recruit him.

"I had done a lot of secular work early in my career," he explains, "so the avenue for secular work is still open to me. But I've made the decision to do gospel music as a ministry.

"You know, I could be out there making money singing jazz and stuff that I love to do. But I've chosen this path and it's a decision that I don't regret. I'm just out there doing what the Lord wants me to do. And all I hope is that I can touch people and help change their lives.

"I want to encourage people, and teach them, and bless them. And I hope through that I can help to save some souls. My music is the vehicle I use, but that's the ultimate purpose of everything I try to do."

Although generally a laid-back person, Daryl gets his hackles up when he begins to discuss the state of the current gospel music industry. What particularly irks him is the impatience he sees among many young gospel artists who are eager to become overnight successes.

"I run into a lot of young people who want to be up onstage and they want to be recording artists and recording stars," he relates. "And they say, 'I want the Lord to anoint me to do so and so and so.'

"But I think it's important that we understand our position and our place among the workings of God, so that we don't become frustrated trying to be something that God has not ordained us to be.

"If you're at a place where you're not feeling that anointing, and there's not a change after you've prayed about it and sought God out, then maybe you need to let loose your dreams and seek out God to see what it is He wants you to do. That's the real secret—to listen to God."

He also becomes irritated by what he perceives as the lack of financial support from fans for gospel music artists.

"It's because they can go to church every Sunday and hear church choirs singing gospel music for free," he angrily submits. "They'll go out and support Anita Baker and Patti and all of that. They go buy their latest albums and don't mind spending forty bucks to see, say, Whitney Houston.

"But when it comes to the lesser-known gospel singers, the attitude is 'if my friend got the album, just tape it for me. I'm not gonna buy that CD; I'm not gonna support that concert, 'cause I can hear that song sung in church.' People a lot of times take professional gospel artists for granted."

As a result, Daryl contends that many gospel artists—himself included—often have a difficult time earning a comfortable living. "You know, I'm convinced that if it wasn't for God, you'd see a lot of gospel singers—who aren't these big secular stars—starving to death.

"That's why I just think it's imperative that we begin to give more support to gospel music, just like we support other art forms out there. Because the other art forms give you something that is temporal or temporary, but gospel music can speak to you from an eternal place."

ALBERTINA WALKER

Photo by Robert Ascroft

While I was a freshman at Tennessee State University, I had the pleasure of being introduced to a Chicago-style gospel singer and her outstanding group, called the Caravans. The gospel singer was Albertina Walker. I am certain that those fan experiences with the Caravans helped me to understand and do what I do in the gospel music industry today.

I hadn't the slightest thought that I'd ever get to meet Albertina Walker, but as fate would have it, she has become one of my closest friends. I have long admired Albertina for her style of singing, especially her "vocal runs." When I invited her to sing on my show and she accepted, we developed a great relationship and it gets stronger each day.

Albertina always made sure that I was kept abreast of all the gospel history that she could stuff into my curious, inquisitive mind. What a joy it is to sit sometimes for hours and listen to her share her amazing stories about the Caravans, the Davis Sisters, the Gospel Harmonettes, Mahalia Jackson, and other legendary gospel artists as they traveled and performed throughout America.

Each incident drew me closer to understanding the sacrifices that the pioneers made. Because of them we do what we do. During these conversations it was revealed that Albertina was certainly touched by God in a wonderful and marvelous way.

The fact that she dropped out of the business for a number of years, and then returned at the request of the late Rev. James Cleveland to continue to bless so many, is a testimony to her faith.

Albertina's greatest fear is that traditional gospel music will be overpowered by the new contemporary styles. She makes sure that when she has a platform with young people, they get the proper and correct information about the development of gospel music.

Albertina is a board member of the various organizations that I've put together to further the growth of gospel music, namely, the Record Label Executives Retreat, the Diamond Festival (a retreat for producers of gospel music television programs), the National Gospel Artists Retreat, and the International Gospel Explosion.

Thank God for Albertina Walker!

$\mathcal{G}$ospel matriarch Albertina Walker's life is a celebration of stamina in a fickle and often harsh world that has tried to knock her down more than once.

The gospel legend's struggles have been many, including a "battle with the devil" over her nicotine habit, and pushing through a prolonged bout of depression that she suffered after the death of her two sisters.

The sixty-eight-year-old Verity Records superstar, who was the protégé and confidante of another gospel legend— Mahalia Jackson—proclaims that despite all her hardships, her heart has never stopped flowing with gratitude toward the Almighty. Her music continues to be an impassioned plea for God to continue to use her as He sees fit.

"I've had plenty of struggles," declares the Grammy Award–winning vocalist, who has recorded more than sixty albums in a career that has spanned four decades.

"But I'm still standing! I'm still here in spite of all that I've been through, and going through, and all. And it's through the grace of God that I came through all of that."

A lifelong resident of Chicago, one of the hotbeds of gospel music, Albertina's personal history reads almost like the story of gospel music itself. In fact, of all the stars in the gospel music firmament, few have shone brighter or more enduringly than this "Queen of Gospel Music," who continues to pack churches and concert halls from coast to coast with her admiring fans.

Albertina's rise to the musical forefront began on the streets of the Windy City. She grew up on Chicago's predominantly black South Side, a working-class neighborhood where families quietly raised their kids and everyone pretty much got along with each other.

"No, it wasn't really bad where I lived," she offers. "It was just an ordinary neighborhood, a family neighborhood where there were buildings filled with families and their children just like my family."

The youngest of nine children, Albertina relates that both her parents were devout Christians, and religion was a subject that was always being discussed at home.

"There was always religion talked about in our house," she declares. "I grew up hearing talk about God's faithfulness. My parents were unashamed to brag on the Lord. But I didn't realize what bein' a Christian was really all about till I was eleven and I got baptized."

Music also filled her household. Albertina's mother, Camilla, a devoutly religious woman and a pillar in the local West Point Baptist Church, could often be found leading the congregational singing.

Much like her talented mother, Albertina also showed musical promise. Before she was even ten, the musically gifted youngster was already singing in church. "God gave that gift to me," she proclaims, "and I just keep hoping it comes out the way He wants it to come out."

Although born with a talent to sing, the gospel legend likes to tell people that she was inspired to sing gospel music because she wanted to be like her mother.

"My mother didn't sing with any musical accompaniment," Albertina recalls, "but she led all the hymns in the church. I used to watch her sing and I admired her. I guess most of my talent comes from her side."

She laughingly describes her father, Reuben, as a man who did not have much of a singing voice. "He was simply a hardworking man who held down different jobs trying to support his large family."

Although never a wild youngster, Albertina recalls with a smile that she did manage to carry on a bit as a teenager. "I didn't party—that wasn't Christ-like," she asserts. "But I did some of the things that teenagers do, except I just didn't go too far out. I was just like any other normal young person."

On those rare occasions when Albertina did step out of line, the gospel great remembers quickly returning to the fold. She was always worried about upsetting her mother or betraying the religious values that her parents had taught her.

"I always felt guilty when I did things that I knew weren't pleasing in the sight of God," she says in that smoky, mesmerizing voice better known for gospel songs. "I was constantly begging for forgiveness because I knew that I was wrong.

"I did a lot of things to see if I really wanted to do those things. But I didn't. They just weren't right for me. So I didn't keep doing them. I said, 'Well, I did that, and I don't like that. So I'll leave this, and I don't want to do that.' What I wanted most of all was to be a follower of Christ; that was the bottom line."

Although religion appealed to her, what really stirred the youngster was the gospel music she heard sung in church. "I just most of all enjoyed singing. I liked religion but I really didn't understand what it was all about until I got a little older."

Sundays in the West Point Baptist Church were always special to her, Albertina recalls. She remembers sitting in church enthralled by the steady stream of noted gospel singers who would sing there, artists like Roberta Martin, Thomas A. Dorsey, and, of course, the great Mahalia, who was always the young girl's favorite. "She used to come to our church to visit and sing there all the time," the prolific singer and songwriter recalls.

"I was just a little girl when I heard Mahalia sing, but I knew right then and there—without a doubt—that's what I wanted to do. That's where I met her. At my own church.

"I used to sit and listen to her sing and talk. I was this little girl she heard sing and took a liking to. And so I grew up around her—I even traveled with her for a while."

Mahalia was so impressed by Albertina's voice that the legendary gospel star eventually took her under her wing, teaching the talented youngster much of what she knew about the craft of singing gospel music.

It wasn't long before the gifted young singer began to emerge in the musical forefront of Chicago's gospel music community. Performing at any church that would have her, and on local radio whenever she had the opportunity, Albertina soon became known for her inspired singing style and powerful voice.

It was a bedrock gospel sound with a voice that was big only when it needed to be. While many of her contemporaries relied on roof-raising dynamics and vocal pyrotechnics to stir their audiences, Albertina, much like her mother had done before her, kept it simple.

She painted a subtle palette of songs in praise to God. And audiences and critics alike responded to this fresh sound with its touches of blues and jazz.

Blessed with a unique voice, the teenager soon found herself invited to perform with gospel groups like the Pete Williams Singers and the Robert Anderson Singers, a popular regional touring act.

But although she was swiftly closing in on the success she sought as a gospel artist, Albertina emphasizes that her religious upbringing always kept her spiritually grounded and down to earth.

"I always was lookin' to have a closer walk with the Lord," she declares. "I'd wanted to live a Christian life since I was eleven years old. That's when I joined the church and got baptized."

That anointing is something that the famed singer recalls "more than anything else in my life." It was during a revival meeting that Albertina decided to devote her life to serving Jesus.

"I went over to this revival. And it was like a spiritual thing that happened to me there," she relates. "I was sitting up in church and I heard this voice say, 'Give your life to the Lord.' It was emotional, you know—a very emotional experience. It was . . ." Albertina gropes for the right words ". . . Holy Ghost–filled. It was an amazing spiritual moment. . . . It was an anointing that the Lord laid on me."

When Albertina left the revival meeting that afternoon, she felt as if she were a brand-new person.

"I was now different from my friends," the gospel great recollects. "I became very religiously inclined, and I tried to stay around people who felt the same way—so I stayed mostly around the church.

"The bottom line is that I was a very, very young girl when that happened. But I grew into grace. When I confessed to Christ, I knew this was the way I wanted to go, the way I wanted to do things. So each day after that I learned a little more about the Lord and Christianity. I had joined the church. I had become a follower of Christ."

As Albertina's reputation as an incredibly talented praise singer continued to grow, her desire to use her voice in bigger and better ways to serve the Almighty also increased.

Such an opportunity presented itself in 1952, when the Robert Anderson Singers ensemble, with whom she had been performing, began to disband. Although Albertina was ready to do something that was creatively different, she remembers not being quite ready to become a solo artist.

"I wanted to be part of an ensemble, because I enjoyed that." Gathering the remaining backup members of the Anderson group, Albertina formed a new ensemble, calling it the Caravans.

From the time of its inception to the group's breakup

in 1966, the Caravans—under her leadership—became the launching pad for some of gospel's greatest talents. Among them were Inez Andrews, Dorothy Norwood, and the Reverend James Cleveland. There was no group in the history of gospel music that produced more stars than this one.

Even when a talented but unknown young singer in the group by the name of Shirley Caesar eventually took over most of the lead vocals from Albertina, the popularity of the Caravans continued.

The group rapidly earned a reputation as the most popular female ensemble in gospel music history, churning out hit songs like "Mary Don't You Weep," "Soldiers in the Army," "The Solid Rock," and "The Blood Will Never Lose Its Power."

In 1966, when Caesar decided to leave the group to pursue evangelism and her own solo career, the other members of the group eventually decided to call it quits.

Albertina folded the Caravans, and finally stepped out to become an artist in her own right. It was from that point on that the acclaimed gospel star's career began to soar to new heights.

A series of number-one hit records followed, along with TV performances and sold-out concerts. Albertina now became recognized as one of gospel music's most influential figures. In 1992, Albertina's popularity soared even further as a result of her knockout appearance in Steve Martin's hit movie *Leap of Faith*.

In 1995, after being nominated eleven times, Albertina won her first Grammy Award. In 1996, she received yet another Grammy nomination for Best Traditional Soul Gospel Album.

Behind her storybook rise to success, there is a subtext in which this premier female vocalist endured against all the odds. One of those challenging times took place just before Albertina gained attention as one of gospel's best, most versatile artists.

"I wanted to be a gospel singer real bad," she recollects, "and I knew the Lord always provided. But I wasn't doing as well back then as I'm doing now. And it was a real struggle.

"Singing wasn't something I ever regretted. So I never turned on the Lord for not doing for me what he did for other people—I was never mad at the Lord," she emphasizes.

" 'Cause I was always a firm believer that God was gonna bless me and do what He wanted to do for me. I always knew the Lord would provide. But it was still difficult."

Despite her belief that she would someday succeed, Albertina's career had come to a virtual standstill. Other gospel artists were getting record contract deals, and she was not. A bit discouraged, she nonetheless kept the faith.

"I was never envious or jealous of anybody—what they had or what they did," she says with emphasis. "Sure I didn't have the success they had, but it turned out that the Lord blessed me, anyway."

Albertina's faith was, again, tested in a struggle she waged to quit the smoking habit. To this very day, the accomplished entertainer believes that habit was inspired by the devil.

"The devil is awfully powerful, you know, and you can really get messed up with him," she says warningly. "And I was afraid of him. That's what happened with smoking. I was smoking since I was a teenager and I wanted to stop. And I couldn't do it on my own."

Then in her forties, Albertina geared herself for one final battle against Satan. The legendary singer recalls falling down on her knees and asking God to make her a victor in her renewed effort to conquer this bad habit. And her prayers were answered.

"I asked the Lord to do it for me, and He did," she jubilantly exclaims. "I prayed and I prayed and I asked the Lord to take that habit away from me and He did. It was a miracle to me!

"The need just went away. It was like I was touched by God because he answered my prayers. And I haven't touched a cigarette or felt the need to smoke since then. It was through the grace of God that I came through that."

Then life pulled the rug out from beneath her in 1984, when two of her sisters died. Albertina reacted by slipping into a deep state of depression. "That really got the best of me," she declares.

"I just didn't know what to do or how to do it. I was feeling depressed and kind of sick. And I didn't think that I was going to make it—but I'm still here. The Lord showed me the way. He led me and guided me through it all. I didn't think I could stand the storm, but He gave me the strength to endure. I don't think I could've made it without Him."

It was through prayer that Albertina recalls eventually overcoming her depression. "I remember that I prayed and asked the Lord for strength to endure.

"But you've got to really know the Lord in order to come in contact with Him on that level. You've got to believe in Him and trust Him, not for just this one thing, but for all things.

"And He heard my prayers. I came out of it because He wanted me to come out of it. He just made the way for me. So in spite of all I was going through at the time, He still brought me through.

"And that's why all I've ever done in my life is praise Him constantly. That never gets old with me. God has given it all to me: past, present, and future. It's all from Him."

Looking back, Albertina believes that all her trials and tribulations have made her a stronger, more faith-driven person. "Oh, yeah, I've had struggles, lots of 'em," she declares like a soldier bragging about his war wounds. "But through the grace of God, I came through them. I trust Him more than ever. And I pray that He continues to use me as He sees fit.

"That's what my song 'I'm Still Here' is about. It's a thank-you song to the Lord for getting me through those struggles. I couldn't have made it without Him. And in spite of all I've been through—and am going through—I'm still here."

Prayer is a word that crops up often in any conversation with this gifted songstress. Albertina reveals she does much of it.

"I don't have a certain time when I pray," she offers. "I pray sometimes in my car and sometimes when I'm walking. I just pray anytime and try to be prayerful all the time, because I can't make it without Him."

Her prayers are of a wide-ranging nature, she discloses. "I pray for more faith and I pray for grace and for Him to make me a better person. I pray for Him to teach me how to love my neighbors and I pray for my friends—and even for my enemies. And I pray for knowledge to understand. I pray for Him to be with me in everything that I say and do."

The difficulties this gospel music superstar has endured over the years have not hardened her spirit. Still warm, endearing, and totally without pretensions, Albertina humbly suggests that all the blessings God has bestowed upon her are available to anyone who seeks Him out.

"The most important step is to read the Word," she advises. "Prayer is the key to it all. You have a choice, you know. You either want to follow Him or follow the devil.

"I always wanted to be on His side. So just meditate, pray, and tune in to what He wants. Follow the Lord. And then wait and listen to what He wants you to do."

Today, the twice-married entertainer, whose first husband died in 1989, continues to call Chicago her home. On almost any weekend, this inspired musical messenger can still be found singing in the choir of her lifelong church.

Looking ahead, the vital and vibrant performer believes that only the Lord knows what is in store for her.

"Whatever the Lord wants me to do—whatever he chooses for me—that's what I'm willing to do. I hope that whenever the Lord chooses to call me home, it can just be said that I fought a good fight, that I finished my course and the Lord is pleased with the life I've lived."

JOHN P. KEE

Photo by Rusty Rust

John P. Kee is called the "Crown Prince of Gospel," and rightfully so. When John came on the scene about ten years ago, I was awed by his remarkable talent, which reminded me of the work of such artists as Andrae Crouch and the Hawkins Family.

I developed a very positive relationship with John as he became part of my television ministry. I will never forget the time when he came and made a sizable donation to the Bobby Jones Gospel Ministry. That was the first time an artist had ever made a financial contribution. I was overwhelmed!

Each time he would come to the stage, the audiences would just go berserk and we all loved it. John usually closed the show, and all the artists would come onstage and participate with him and the New Life Community Choir simply because they loved his music and his style.

John's choir would always exhibit a great deal of maturity and commitment to their leader. Even though his group would change members from time to time, he would always keep that good John Kee sound.

I am very proud to see that John has opened a church in Charlotte, North Carolina, and has a tremendous street ministry. It takes a brave soldier to go to the streets and talk about Jesus. John is not ashamed to tell you that he has been touched by God.

$\mathcal{A}$t one point in his life John drifted so far into the high-living lifestyle of drugs, easy money, and getting high that he operated a small grocery store in Charlotte, North Carolina, that was actually a front for drug trafficking.

For the North Carolina teenager, the fast lane nearly proved to be his demise. It was also a hard-core lifestyle far different from how his God-fearing parents had raised him.

But the reformed drug dealer–turned–God's warrior, whose powerful stage persona and charismatic style often reminds his fans of the legendary Rev. James Cleveland, eventually grew weary of the senseless violence that surrounded him—capped off by the shooting death of a close friend in a drug deal gone wrong.

That was when the Verity Records star, founder of one of today's most popular gospel groups—the New Life Community Choir—decided to turn his life around.

Today, it is no longer drugs that the award-winning musician and pastor is selling, but something much more beneficial for anyone wanting to get high: the promise of redemption through the love of Jesus Christ.

"God called me for a purpose, and when I finally recognized that, many good things started to happen," he proclaims. "I had faltered and I fell, but God helped me to stand right back up."

One of sixteen children, John was reared on the outskirts of Durham, North Carolina, until he was five. Then, seeking employment opportunities, the family relocated to the city where John's father, John Henry Kee, found work as a foreman at a brickyard, and his mother, Lizzie Mae, earned a living as a registered nurse.

Reminiscing about his childhood, John doesn't recall the neighborhood he grew up in as a particularly tough one.

"As kids we didn't know anything about tough neighborhoods. Every kid took care of his own at that time," he explains. "We didn't have the guns, the knives, the violence back then. You were a young man, you handled yourself."

He describes his upbringing as a "wonderful childhood. We didn't know we were poor because we were a very happy family. We really had lots of joy in that family and we learned to appreciate good values at an early age.

"Sure there were lots of challenges, but I guess God blessed us and allowed us to achieve. So I can't really describe my childhood as a struggle. It was a real blessed family."

The acclaimed gospel artist recalls that there were "ten girls, six boys, mother, father, grandpa, grandma. It was a large family and we were all raised together. I was the fifteenth child, and the last of the six boys."

And because he was the last son, John remembers that his biggest struggle at that early age was trying to get his fair share of his father's attention—which he usually was able to do by playing the piano.

"Anything that had to do with music would capture his attention," John says, smiling. "He had a gospel choir

in the late forties, early fifties called the Southland Gospel
Singers. We could all sing, but I was the only one who
could also play."

The subject of the old piano always comes up when
John talks about his childhood. "It was an old Walter's
upright grand that I now have stored in my home," he
says. "I challenged myself to play a few chords by ear,
and that's how this whole piano thing started.

"I was about seven years old when I started playing
that piano, and I got a lot of encouragement because
music in our household was just the thing to do. And it
was by playing piano that I kept my dad's attention. I
knew he loved music, so I kind of had an edge."

Besides being rooted in music, John grew up with a
knowledge of the Bible. Both of his parents were devoutly
religious and avid churchgoers.

"It was a very religious home. My grandmother was
like a backbone." He laughs. "There was Sunday morning
prayer, eight o'clock prayer, Scripture reading during the
week, and then the family sang. We had a little gospel
thing going around the house twenty-four hours a day.

"I guess that was the start of my love for gospel
music. It was growing up in that household. It kind of
moved me forward to the career that I ended up with. I
guess this was the way God allowed me to achieve what I
have accomplished in my later years. That's why I say it
was a real blessed family."

There is a more personal reason why John believes he
has soared to such professional heights, one that has
earned the talented performer the title of the "Crown
Prince of Gospel." It has to do with his late father.

"My dad died in 1981, and I believe that I actually
carried his vision out," John reflects. "He had a record
deal in New York in the early to midfifties. But because of
the prejudices in the South at that time, he couldn't
accomplish his dream.

"It was kind of discouraging for him not to be allowed to play here or there. He wasn't even allowed to have his bus with his choir pass through Virginia because his choir was all black. That's why he was very proud of my gospel career. He wanted me to carry out the vision that he started."

While John is pleased to have been able to fulfill his father's expectations for him, he remains saddened that for so long a period of time he let himself down.

"Looking back at my life I see that I really got side-tracked," the award-winning singer and producer declares. "I still knew how to pray, and I always remembered how I was raised, but I was living in sin."

It was the enormous talent that John demonstrated at an early age vocally and on the piano that in many ways contributed to his downfall, he explains. "I was raised right, but I left North Carolina after I graduated. I graduated high school very early.

"Somebody noticed, around age eleven or something, that I had this little gift for piano playing—I was playing by ear. And I was a lover of classical music," he offers, laughing.

"A lot of people don't even have a clue that's true about me, but I would actually travel around the county in an opera called *The Toymaker*. And I was the toymaker. And here I was this young kid about eleven or twelve."

Graduating at age fourteen from the North Carolina School of the Arts in Winston-Salem, he eventually ended up at the Yuba College Conservatory of Music in northern California, where he majored in music.

"So at fifteen years old, I was in California, living the life of an adult. And I think that was really one of the ills," he contends. "Before I was really able to capture or recognize who I was, I already had the challenges of being an adult: I was paying rent by myself and driving a car without a license."

While at college, John helped to support himself by playing gigs with a number of jazz notables like Donald Byrd and the Blackbyrds, and Cameo. His talented work with these groups was already beginning to bring him public attention.

But that lifestyle also swept him into the fast-paced world of drugs and money. "It started when I was playing a lot of those jazz sessions," he recollects. "And then after California, well, I got involved with the Miss Black Universe pageants. My job was to train the voices.

"That job got me to Charlotte, where I started working with an agency called GM Productions, and that's where the drug thing really started to happen. I started buying and selling drugs, and I was working out of a grocery store near the projects in a neighborhood called Double Oaks."

Still only in his late teens, John recalls that the illegal operation was so lucrative that he and his friends were pulling in thousands of dollars weekly. "I started out selling a little marijuana from behind the counter, and it just evolved. It kind of grew into a major deal because I had such a good cover." The concept of using a grocery store as a front to sell drugs came while he was dating the daughter of the woman who owned the store, John recalls.

"So I started working there and the store started doing double the business. The woman and her daughter never knew what I was up to," he adds, laughing. "They were loving it! This great salesman had come to town.

"And the truth of the matter is—and I'll never forget this—one Fourth of July the store made $2,000 before noon! It wasn't grocery store money when she closed out the cash register, it was drug money. But she didn't know the difference."

Although he sold drugs, John is careful to emphasize that he never got himself involved in any violence pertaining to his illicit employment. "I didn't live the thug life. I mean, it wasn't like I was working the streets," he asserts.

"My cover was the grocery store. I was moving a lot of money, and I was moving a lot of paper. I was about seventeen or eighteen at the time, although I was telling people that I was twenty-three or twenty-four."

John honestly admits that he soon started using drugs himself. "I wasn't a major user," he declares. "But I got involved with a little cocaine, and I was a pot smoker. But I didn't call that major. I wasn't hung out there. But the cocaine did get a little out of hand near the end. It got a little strong."

In his early twenties, John began to feel that his life had somehow gotten out of control. The senseless violence that surrounded him became intolerable, and the money and cars and whatever other material gains his drug dealing was earning him no longer seemed to provide any solace.

"A friend of mine got killed, and that friend was very close," he relates. "He died for a little bit of money, and it could have been me. So I started saying around this time—it was '81 or '82—that I didn't want to die on the streets.

"I was seeing young men dying on the street, and I think I just made up my mind that I did not want to leave here like that. I just felt like there was a gift or something inside of me, and I didn't want to waste it.

"To tell you the truth, although I gained knowledge about what salvation was when I joined Jim Bakker's PTL revivals later on, I gave my life to the Lord the night I saw the brother get killed. It was a major turning point. I honestly believe that."

John also feared letting down his father, who had recently died. "Even before he died I just never wanted him to know what I was doing," he submits. "But I think he really knew what I was up to. He had been to the store a couple of times, and that shook me up."

It was in the midst of this intolerable situation that the acclaimed musician believes he was touched by God. "I call it the renaissance period where I recognized what deliverance really is," he asserts.

"It was then that I made up my mind that I wanted to be delivered. It was awesome that once I made my mind up to do something, it almost immediately happened.

"That's why I think my testimony is so strong. It shows that once you actually do the things you make up your mind to do—like seeking deliverance—you can be delivered."

The first thing John remembers doing in his search for salvation was seeking out a choir.

"I started working with a small inner-city choir in Charlotte. They were some people who were not really popular in gospel music, and they called themselves the Combination Choir. They were kids like me, kids whose lives took a dramatic turn when they surrendered to Christ.

"And through them I met a young lady by the name of Beverly Crouch. And she really ministered to my heart. I was around the right people just when I decided to change my life. It was awesome.

"I was around some Christians who were rooted and grounded in Jesus, and that meant a lot to me. I actually saw people being saved in my presence. By being around them, I saw some hands-on examples of what God can really do."

In return for the love he received from his new friends, John began to train the choir in all the musical techniques he had studied over the years.

"I took all the music training that I knew—the voice training that I had acquired from the North Carolina School of the Arts—and I was able to sit down and train this group of people who were just singing *a cappella* all those years."

It was through the urging of his new friends that John agreed to attend one of Jim and Tammy Bakker's PTL revivals. It was a visit that would go a long way toward accelerating his own religious revival.

"Jim had a park on PTL grounds called Buffalo Park," he recalls. "Jim and Tammy had their church there at the time. So I would go to that church on Sundays. It was the kind of church where I didn't have to be anyone special. I didn't even have to wear a tie.

"I could actually just go and sit down and receive the Word and take Jesus into my heart. And, as a young Christian, it was real good for me because the Sunday service was not like the TV program.

"It wasn't about finances or keeping the cameras rolling. It was just Sunday services, and it was real positive for me. So I'll always be grateful in my heart for this little choir letting me know where the PTL grounds were."

Soon, John was a regular at those revival meetings. "I wanted to become spiritual and deep, and fulfill my calling," he recollects. "So I actually started going to PTL revivals and I gave my heart to Jesus at one of those revivals. I even had a chance to throw my arms around Jim Bakker's neck and tell him, 'Thank you.' He encouraged my spirit and turned me around for the better."

Talking about the fate that Jim and Tammy suffered still saddens the gospel star. John is particularly regretful that he wasn't there to lend the couple his moral support when they were carted off to prison in handcuffs.

"It was Jim's church that gave meaning to my experience of finding Jesus," John proclaims. "I learned Scripture there—the Bible was always open. I really learned to read Scripture at his church.

"That's why it was one of my most painful moments to see him on television being carried off. I wasn't there to judge him and I would never judge him. I wish I had been there that day to tell him: 'Listen, I've been a follower of your music. I know who you are. If it had not been for you, I wouldn't have received the kinds of experiences that I did.' "

Today, the musician and pastor of his own flourishing church reflects that while his friend's death was certainly a crucial turning point in his spiritual life, he believes that God was busy working on him long before that.

"I think the touching came even before then—and I teach this now, as a pastor," he submits. "I teach that even in your sins and what you are going through before you make that decision to really come to the Lord, the Lord's hand is in your life.

"These near misses—these almost deaths—that's not luck or some type of fantasy. That's the Lord telling you that He has something in store for you. And I think it's good to recognize that before you get hit by the truck, if you know what I mean. I lot of people get hit by a truck or shot at, and it's only then that they say, 'Oh, God had something he wanted to change in me.' But I recognized he wanted me to change early on."

That knowledge, he explains, was an intuition that John believes stemmed from a special contract between him and the Lord. "I think it has to do with my contract—and I don't mean my recording contract," he says, smiling.

"I really mean my covenant with God. I think there was some kind of divine destiny that I be a singer. Because here I am the only son named after my father, who also loved gospel music."

The power of John's ministry has always been fueled by his love of gospel music. "When I sing a gospel song I feel like I'm ministering," he declares. "There was even a time in '79, '80, when I had a jazz program in a lot of the black colleges. But after I left the stage, all I felt was that I had stopped playing. I wasn't high off the music. Gospel always presented some message to my core. I would go home and sing "Glory to His Name" to myself and really enjoy it."

John's own star began to rise in the 1980s, when the Combination Choir grew and blossomed into the New Life Community Choir, with the talented musician as its leader.

While leading the ensemble, which eventually signed a major label recording contract, John also wrote hit songs for such gospel luminaries as Daryl Coley, the Hawkins Family, and the Reverend James Cleveland.

The young artist's career accelerated in 1985 when John became the first artist to record lead vocals on two selections for the Gospel Music Workshop of America's annual mass choir recording.

"I was the first gospel artist to ever write more than one song for that convention," he proudly states. "So I made gospel history on that and doors began to open. Things started to happen very, very fast."

John went on to write and record "Jesus Loves Me" for the Edwin Hawkins Music & Arts Seminar Album, *Give Us Peace,* which resulted in a demo that John personally financed.

That demo, featuring his choir singing behind him, eventually led to a record contract in 1987 with a small label, Tyscot Records, and a debut album for the gospel artist, *Wait on Him.* That was to be the first of fourteen albums that John and his choir would record in the years to come.

With a trophy case full of Stellar, GMWA, and Soul Train Music Awards, the gospel star could easily have basked in all his personal acclaim and achievement. Instead, he remembers undergoing a period of doubt and a serious challenge to his faith.

It was shortly after his 1995 certified gold album,

Show Up!, and his follow-up 1996 smash hit, *Stand!*, when the musician and minister began to question his calling and his ability to write any more songs of spiritual worth.

"I was fatigued and searching for God's will," he recalls. "I started to wonder, Am I through? Is this it? Is there something else for me to say? Are people still listening to what I say?"

One night, while in meditation on his tour bus, John recalls receiving an answer to his soul-searching questions. "I was thinking about all of this and I started hearing the Lord's voice. It was amazing . . . it was awesome. I felt like I was touched.

"And He really reaffirmed to me that He had called me for a purpose—and it wasn't about how many people were listening to me. And that stuck with me. And since that moment wonderful things began to happen.

"He just put the power into my pen and the songs started coming. He gave me the strength I needed. He let me know that He was not finished with me yet. A lot of the songs on my new album, *Strength!*, are about divine intervention."

John says what he learned from that experience is that "you're not on your own. You're on a divine assignment. And just because you have doubts or fall on your face, it doesn't mean that your assignment has been canceled."

Looking toward the future, John holds a vision that goes far beyond awards and more records.

"There's so much hurting and suffering in the world," he proclaims, "and the only way not to be overwhelmed by it is to know that you're doing something about it."

John hopes that through his church ministry he can help work toward relieving some of that pain in the years to come. "Our church is reaching out to the community with tutors for schoolkids, food for the hungry, shelter for the homeless and elderly," he says proudly.

"My dream is that one day the entire gospel community will reach out as one to show the love of Christ to those who need it the most. That means more to me than awards, and deals, and business. That's the business of the Lord, and that's what I'm here to accomplish."

The inspired musical messenger also hopes that his music continues to play a role in inspiring the needy—regardless of age, background, or denomination.

"Every album I've recorded has been done with the conscious intention of capturing the heart and mind of everyone from the baby to the grandma," he declares.

"I want to tear the categorizations apart and then put them back together in a way that creates a new musical common denominator—music that brings people into oneness in worship."

Because of his own experience on the streets of Durham as a former drug dealer, one of John's special missions is to reach out to Charlotte's hard-core drug traffickers and other troubled youth in his community to try and dissuade them from such a lifestyle.

Toward this end, on almost any Sunday morning the musician and pastor can be found performing in his church for local teens in a show that combines a hip-hop and urban sound with a gospel message.

"It's music that crosses barriers," he explains. "The kids are moving to it, but so are their parents and grandmas. I'm blessed to be that kind of catalyst for people. It's speaking to their heart, mind, and spirit."

John says he is also working hard to improve the community itself, especially the area where he once worked the drug trade. "You know the store that I sold drugs at? Well, a couple of years ago I went back and purchased all the land that surrounded the project area.

That's where we're building our new church and our church school.

"We're developing seventeen acres for major businesses to rotate that dollar right in that same neighborhood where I once sold drugs. And I'm also trying to buy the store. I want to stand on that site and see that I'm doing something good with it. I want to minister to the needs of that community."

Another aspect of John's youth outreach ministry is a special project, the Victory in Praise Music & Arts Convention, which he organized in 1990. The annual event attracts some two thousand young choir members to Charlotte, where they are provided with fellowship, encouragement, and an opportunity to meet some of the industry's top gospel stars.

"I wanted to make sure that the young people I see getting saved realize that victory isn't just for thirty minutes or an hour while I'm onstage, but to let them know that victory can be a permanent part of their life," he declares with heartfelt sincerity.

Turning to the subject of the state of the gospel music industry today, John shows a touch of annoyance. "I'm not really bitter, but I don't see the love we used to have," he contends.

"It's because of that I'm thinking about taking a break from performing. I'd still produce other groups and do special projects, but I'm really burned out with the industry."

John attests that what ticks him off the most is the attitude among many young gospel stars that they are willing to do anything if only they can become overnight sensations.

"And that's been very painful to see, because we're supposed to be committed to God," he declares. "We're supposed to have that covenant or that contract with Christ, and there should be some boundaries or something set that says, 'Hey, I will do this, but I won't do that.'

"I've seen artists lie, connive, cut throats—not from the back, but from the front—just to make it. And that's really scary, because that's not the type of people we're supposed to be."

The versatile vocalist believes that the gospel music industry could also learn much by studying the secular music industry. "These secular artists seem to get along," he asserts. "They work together. Their companies are not feuding the way we are so that they can't sing together.

"There should be many more records with gospel artists coming together, singing together. But the companies are afraid of who's going to make the most money."

John confides that when he watched the recent Stellar Awards telecast it was a bit unsettling. "I couldn't pinpoint anything to individualize us. I understand the contemporary sound—I have one myself. But nowadays I've started to ask myself questions about where this industry is going. We used to have much more commitment to each other and the ministry."

John, who lives with his new wife, Felice, and nineyear-old daughter, Myeesha, in Charlotte, says he has much to be grateful for, especially the Lord's forgiveness for the mistakes he has made over the years.

That same forgiveness is available to anyone who turns to Jesus Christ, he submits.

"I think that we all need to understand that He was as tempted as we are—as I once was. For years as a child growing up in a church, I heard that Scripture, and it would stop right there.

"I think we have to instill in our babies and our kids and those that want to walk with God, that our walk with the Lord is not over because we've sinned. We're going to have to learn that we can live a delivered life—and it doesn't mean you're not going to falter, that you're not going to fall."

John pauses for a moment. "You have a right to stand back up," he continues. "I'm excited about that because that's our message. Jesus was challenged by the same temptations that we are. We have a high priest who forgives our infirmities."

DOROTHY NORWOOD

Photo by Kriegsman Photography, New York

I first became familiar with Dorothy when I listened to her album *Johnny and Jesus*. I began to read about her past association with the Caravans. I met Dorothy later on and we became good friends.

I marveled at her ability to capture experiences from her past and put some of those experiences into story form and record them. Then I noticed how well she could reach out to her audiences. Her ability to relate to her fans of many lifestyles and persuasions was absolutely mind-blowing.

In my conversations with Dorothy, I realized that she played a major role in developing and continuing positive relationships within her family. Dorothy became the center of stability for her brothers and sisters and was madly in love with Hattie B., her mom.

Dorothy also has high regard for the pioneers of gospel music. Even today, she keeps Albertina Walker by her side in all her endeavors. She has never forgotten what Albertina did for her when she selected her for her group, the Caravans.

Now, what really impresses me about Dorothy, other than her musical acumen, is her business savvy. She began producing other artists, setting up her companies, and touring the nation in search of gospel music–related adventures. She has become quite successful with all of her enterprises.

Dorothy's outward "Praise to God" is evidence of her relationship with Him. She will stop, at the drop of a hat, and, amidst her singing and storytelling ministry, give vent to the Holy Spirit. What joy it is to observe one of those anointed moments.

God bless Dorothy Norwood!

$\mathcal{S}$he had gone from touring with the Rolling Stones and performing before packed houses of sixty thousand or more people, to preaching, singing, and selling her tapes at local churches in order to support herself.

But during those "lean" years, the "Queen of Gospel Music," who was first touched by God when she was only thirteen years old, never once became embittered toward the Lord.

The seasoned gospel veteran and six-time Grammy nominee, who experienced a second, even more intense moment with God at age twenty-six, believes she was able to endure those discouraging years because of her unshakable faith in the Lord.

Today, the sixty-year-old singer and evangelist, who over the course of her thirty-six-year professional career has performed with such gospel greats as Mahalia Jackson, the Reverend James Cleveland, and Albertina Walker, is as popular as ever. Dorothy continues to be one of gospel's dominant figures.

Described by many as the "world's greatest gospel story-teller," the Malaco Records star just recently released her forty-third album: *Hattie B's Daughter*.

In it, she pays tearful tribute to her mother, who introduced her to the Word of God, and offers special thanks to the Lord for bringing her through all of her life's trials and tribulations.

"God has preserved me to do my work for Him, so why shouldn't I praise Him?" the Georgia native proclaims with heartfelt emotion. "You've just got to believe in what you don't even see yet. You can't give up on your faith, because if you lose your faith you're gonna sink."

The daughter of a Baptist preacher and a choir director, Dorothy reminisces that it was nearly impossible for her not to be deeply affected by religion and music.

"With my dad being a preacher, I grew up in a very strict religious household where we were in church every Sunday," she recalls. "And that was just a blessing for me to be brought up like that, because we sang the gospel, and we heard the Word every Sunday."

Her father, the Reverend R. F. Norwood, was such a devout Christian that she and her four siblings were not even allowed to attend neighborhood dances, she recollects.

"We were a very religious family," she asserts. "We were dedicated to the church and spent most of our time in church. That was my life. I knew nothing different. We didn't go out and dance on the ballroom floors and hang out."

As the middle one of five children—three sisters and a brother—what Dorothy remembers the most about the suburban Atlanta, Georgia, neighborhood in which she was raised was the beautiful house that her family lived in.

"We weren't a rich family, but we were able to survive without being in poverty," the acclaimed gospel star recalls. "What we had was a very nice house. When he wasn't preaching my dad worked as a carpenter. I was six years old and I can still clearly recall him working on that house. God blessed us with that house."

When Dorothy turns to the subject of her mother, to whom she was deeply devoted, a note of sadness enters her voice. "Her name was Hattie B. and she was a singer," she relates in the storyteller voice for which she has become famous.

"And she worked as a cook for white people, and they would give her their used designer clothes. She started a business with those clothes: her own resale shop. On my latest recording I tell the entire story about Hattie B."

Music was as much part of Dorothy's life as religion, she recalls. At age eight, she was already singing and touring with her musically gifted family.

"My mother and all my sisters sang," Dorothy relates. "Our family had a gospel singing group called the Norwood Gospel Singers. We used to tour from church to church all over the South."

Although church often served as a second home for the youngster, it wasn't until Dorothy was a teen that religion took on a special significance for her. It was at that age when Dorothy believes she was first touched by God.

Even today, that moment remains a special one for her. "It's something in my life that I'll never forget," she declares. "I remember it was a warm Sunday morning and I was about thirteen years old. I had walked into the Mt. Vernon Baptist Church in Atlanta for a regular service, and I was singing a song."

In the midst of that song, Dorothy remembers suddenly feeling as if she were being filled with light and warmth. "The Lord just filled me with his Holy Spirit," she proclaims. "It happened all of a sudden right in the middle of that song. It was an incredible experience.

"I mean, I'll never forget it. I was just so filled with the feeling of God's anointment. It was then and there that I dedicated my whole life to the Lord. And then things began to change for me."

One of the most obvious changes was in her singing voice. "I just all of a sudden started to sing better," she declares. "It was like the anointing that fell upon me had changed my voice. Now every time I sang, people would just shout and get happy. It was miraculous.

"My mother began to notice it and my father began to notice it. Even when I was singing in our group, people were just so *touched*. It was just a blessing to me."

Reflecting back upon that occasion, Dorothy considers it a major turning point in her life, a moment in which the talented youngster first decided that she wanted to become a gospel singer.

"He not only filled me with the Holy Spirit, but it was then that I knew my calling. I wanted to praise God through my music. My life began to unfold for me right there and then."

When Dorothy left the church that afternoon, she felt like a completely different person. She recollects that even her parents noticed the change in her.

"They always talked about what had happened to me that day. They would not only talk to me about it, but to their friends and neighbors. And they would testify about it in church. They thought it was kind of miraculous."

Dorothy agreed. "Yes, I thought it was sort of miraculous. But I felt it deeper than my parents did, because it was my experience. I knew that God had given me a calling in life: to use my voice to minister to people. It was just a blessing to be able to walk closer with the Lord. Although I had been in church all my life, this was a new experience for me."

That fervor for the Lord continued all the way through high school, Dorothy recalls. "In high school, people sensed that there was something special about me.

"Whether it was in the glee club or some other activity, I'd always sing a gospel song. And the minute I began singing people would be drawn to me. They'd gather around me. They loved it."

By 1956, the talented youngster had moved to Chicago to pursue her ambition to become a gospel artist. Word spread quickly through the Windy City's gospel community about the teenager with the remarkable voice.

Soon, Dorothy found herself singing with such gospel notables as the great Mahalia Jackson, and the incomparable Rev. James Cleveland. She also won a position with the Caravans, one of gospel's most legendary groups, which was then headed up by gospel great Albertina Walker.

"James was my mentor," Dorothy submits. "I grew up under James and in later years I worked with him, singing in his group. He was such a great influence, a person after my own heart. His music was not compromised. He was a great, great artist."

Compromise was not Dorothy's style either. Whether she was singing as part of James Cleveland's choir or, in later years, leading her own group, the heart and soul of Jesus could always be heard in Dorothy's music. Always, the young singer who had been touched by God expressed her deep love of the Lord through the lyrics of her songs.

In 1964 Dorothy launched her solo career, capturing national attention with her first Savoy Records album, *Johnny and Jesus*. Reviewers raved about her "bone-chilling inspirational voice," and the album was certified gold.

Another smash hit followed: the stirring *Denied Mother*. That album also went gold. On the album, her singular gift for recitation quickly earned Dorothy the title of the "World's Greatest Storyteller."

Although the twenty-nine-year-old gospel singer already felt as if she were sitting on top of the world, Dorothy would soon go to further heights as a result of a second remarkable religious experience.

That transformational moment took place one summer during a revival meeting in Columbia, South Carolina.

"I remember that I was driving to the A. A. Allen Revival, and I was supposed to be one of the featured performers," Dorothy testifies. "When I got there, the revival was already going on. There was singing and there was preaching going on."

Dorothy recalls she was completing her song when things began to get a bit wild. "I remember the preacher saying that 'anyone wants the Holy Ghost should run to the tent.' There was another small tent for people who wanted to be touched by the Holy Ghost."

What happened next still remains something of a blur to her. What she can clearly recall is that "all of a sudden I found myself running to that tent. I ran into that tent and I fell on my knees. And, oh, the spirit of the Lord just came.

"It was a moment—an experience—in my life that I'll never forget," Dorothy exults. "It was like time had stopped for me. I fell on my knees and people came into the tent and they started praying for me. And that's when I started speaking in tongues."

Dorothy pauses to savor that memory. "I couldn't stop speaking in tongues," she recalls. "I went back to the hotel that night and I couldn't even stay in bed, I was so filled with the Lord. I was walking up and down the street thinking about my experience.

"I was saved when I was thirteen years old and received Christ in the Baptist Church. But when I went to this Holiness Church—it's really called the Church of God in Christ—it was a whole new dimension."

Today, reflecting upon that experience, Dorothy credits it to a lifetime of "being dedicated to the Lord. I had dedicated myself to God when I was thirteen, but I always wanted to get closer.

"There was something that I was reaching for even though I had been saved for a long time. I wanted to go to a higher level with the Lord, and that's what happened to me."

She recalls that in the weeks that followed, "all of a sudden these incredible things started happening to me. I got a new recording contract and, in 1972, I started traveling with Mick Jagger and the Rolling Stones. I was now a bigger star than ever before. And I had also become an evangelist."

The Rolling Stones tour is a memory she cherishes to this very day. Dorothy still remembers how during the thirty-state tour she often found herself performing before audiences in excess of sixty thousand people.

Despite the often raucous atmosphere in the stadiums and concert halls where the Rolling Stones appeared, whenever she took the stage a respectful hush would fall over the crowd, the faith-driven gospel star recollects.

Peering out from the stage at the sea of faces before her, Dorothy remembers thinking how blessed she was that the daughter of a Baptist preacher and a choir director was being given this opportunity to spread God's Word.

"Now I was able to spread the gospel in a mission field that was virtually closed to gospel artists. It was just wonderful," she exclaims. "You could see them crying when I did 'Johnny and Jesus,' and they loved 'When the Saints Go Marching In.' And Mick Jagger was such a great guy. I'd see him watching me perform. I was singing and telling stories."

By now, Dorothy's fame as a gospel singer had spread beyond the United States. She found herself touring Europe and playing to standing-room-only houses in Germany, France, Sweden, Denmark, Holland, and England. It was a nonstop roller coaster ride until about 1985, when the lean years began to set in.

"Between 1985 and 1991 I found myself without a recording contract, but I was managing to remain afloat," she recalls. "My record company had gone out of business.

"I was living in the New York area, up in Harlem, and I was singing mostly at church services and concerts. But it wasn't anything like it was when I was traveling out there with the Rolling Stones."

Dorothy, who had recently become an ordained minister, remembers how she often had to peddle her tapes in churches in order to earn money. As discouraging as it was, she always kept her spirits up.

"I never ever lost my faith," she proudly asserts. "I knew that God would take me through this. I knew that, in the end result, I was going to come out victorious. I just knew that if I gave up on my faith that I would sink. So I never lost it, even through those hard times.

"There were times when I would get down to my last cent, and something would always come through for me. And I didn't just sit around and wait for something to happen."

She relates one story to illustrate how, despite the difficult time she was going through, God still remained by her side. "It's just one of a lot of stories I can tell you about how He's just been with me," she exclaims.

"I had come up with the vision that I wanted to do a reunion concert with the Caravans. I was really out of money and I met this man—Joe Long—who was with a small record company in Brooklyn.

"And I brought all the Caravans to New York and they came without even asking for a deposit. I collaborated with Joe and he put up the money for the promotion.

"So we packed two sold-out concerts in Brooklyn and Newark on a Saturday and a Sunday. And the proceeds from those two concerts were tremendous. We managed to walk away with almost $20,000 each after we paid everything off."

For Dorothy, the success of this venture was nothing less than a miracle, one, she believes, that came about as the result of having kept her faith in God.

"He came through for me. He took me through it," she says with emphasis. "But I now also decided not to just sit and wait for Him to do something else for me. I decided to do something on my own."

With the proceeds from the Caravans concert, Dorothy packed her suitcase and left for California with a plan in mind. If no label was interested in signing her to record an album, then she would finance and produce one of her own.

"I had faith in this recording," she submits. "So I took my money and I went to Oakland, California, and I paid for a recording session. I did all this through faith.

"I got the best musicians and one of the best choirs— because I knew, with all my experience, that you can't do anything on a low budget and expect it to compete with what's out there. We used Reverend James Cleveland's musicians."

The result of that recording session was *Dorothy Norwood Live With the Northern California GMWA Choir,* a record that ended up in the hands of the late Frank Williams, then an executive at Malaco Records.

Williams liked what he heard, and by February 1991, the gifted entertainer was Malaco's newest recording artist. "They immediately signed me and we got all the money back we'd spent on it," she says, smiling.

The *Live* album was an immediate hit, and songs like "Victory Shall Be Mine" reached the number one position on the gospel charts after only seven weeks of airplay.

By October of that same year, Dorothy was not only back in the gospel music spotlight, but also found herself on a whirlwind thirty-one-city U.S. concert tour. Her success continued. A follow-up album, *Better Days Ahead,* earned the revitalized performer a Stellar Award as well as a Grammy nomination.

In 1996 and 1997, her fourth project with Malaco, *Shake off the Devil,* earned the acclaimed singer more Stellar, Grammy, and Dove award nominations.

Having shaken off her own devil, Dorothy remains grateful for the Almighty's help in doing so.

"He's stayed with me ever since," she jubilantly proclaims. "My faith was stirred and strengthened as a result of what happened to me, and I felt new depths of trust in God's goodness. I still feel that way."

In a long career of recording more than forty albums, five of which have been certified gold, Dorothy not only continues to reap honors (she was recently inducted into the Gospel Music Hall of Fame), but her wit, wisdom, and passion as an evangelist also keep her in demand on the speaker's circuit.

Wherever she can command an audience—whether it's from the pulpit or before a seminar—Dorothy always stresses the importance of keeping faith with God.

"You've got to believe in what you don't even see yet," she emphasizes. "You've got to know that the Lord is always with you, just as He's always been with me."

Looking ahead, the gospel star, who now lives with her sister in Englewood, New Jersey, hopes to do more to help promote new gospel artists.

She remembers when she, herself, was a young singer and people like Albertina Walker and James Cleveland helped her to get started in the gospel music business.

"That's what I look forward to doing," she declares. "I want to do even more to help other people. I've already produced eleven projects—albums by other artists—and Malaco has signed most of the people that I produced.

"That's my goal. To sing and to preach. To reach out to people who listen to my music and to reach out and help others as someone once helped me. And I want to continue my ministry until the Lord calls me home. I want to do more preaching and praising of the Lord. God has preserved me to do work for Him, why shouldn't I?"

Dorothy confides that prayer is an essential part of her life. "Sometimes I just walk and pray. I also pray riding in my car. I find that you don't always have to get on your knees and pray. But I always stay in touch with the Lord."

Dorothy says she continues to remain grateful for the two times she was touched by God. "Both those times it was God calling on my life and telling me to spread His word," she declares. "And that's why my goal is to continue my ministry until the Lord calls me home."

She also modestly submits that such blessings are available to anyone who seeks out God.

"All you have to do is acknowledge Him in all ways and He'll direct your path," she counsels. "And keep the faith. Don't let go of your faith. If you lose your faith, you've lost out," she proclaims.

MARK KIBBLE

Photo by David Roth

Mark was first introduced to me when he came to sing on my television program. At the time, he was a member of a mixed group called A Special Blend. The group was excellent! Their harmonies were very much like that of Mark's current group, Take 6.

When I realized that Mark had moved to Nashville and put together another group, of all male singers this time, I never thought that this particular ensemble would rise to be a leader in the world of gospel music.

Mark is the force behind the movement. His father, who is a minister, is a big influence in his life and I predict that Mark will end up as a minister and pastor in a few short years.

I feel that Mark has a strong knowledge of how to excite people about Jesus. His stage persona is just right for a soldier to convey his message in this warfare against the enemy.

Mark Kibble is touched by God.

$\mathcal{A}$lthough his seven-time Grammy Award–winning group, Take 6, is acclaimed for its *a cappella*–style harmonies, lead tenor Mark Kibble remembers two disharmonizing periods in his life when the devil manipulated him into a prolonged state of anger instead of Christ-like gentleness.

Mark, the son of a Seventh Day Adventist minister, reacted with anger upon learning that his parents were getting divorced. The Reprise Records star turned to alcohol and other reckless behavior to cope with that anger.

Later, confronted with unfounded accusations about his sexual orientation because several of his college friends were thought to be gay, Mark adopted a "tough guy" persona, angrily turning on both his accusers and his friends.

The New York native believes that in both instances—once with the assistance of what he believes was an angel—the reading of Scripture helped him defeat Satan and overcome his anger.

"That kind of anger and hatred shouldn't be in your life," he declares. "That's something the Lord doesn't want in your life. And it was by reading the Word that I realized that everything should come from the motivation of love, not hate; that God is love and He requires you to love everybody."

As a youngster, Mark remembers moving around a lot. "I was actually born in the Bronx, and my dad was pastoring in New York City at the time," Mark offers. "He was just getting started in the ministry. Then we moved to Long Island, but I can hardly remember what that was like.

"And not too long after that we moved to Bridgeport, Connecticut. Then we moved from Bridgeport to Boston within two years. I remember what that was like." In Boston, the five-year-old got his first glimpse of racial hatred.

"We were around Boston when all the racial riots were going on." To this day, the acclaimed singer, raised on heart-warming messages about God's love, still has some disturbing memories of the negative atmosphere that swelled all around him.

"That was my first racial experience," he declares. "I can actually still remember my dad taking me to some of those hearings, and then us having to leave the city because it was getting so violent," he relates. "We lived in a neighborhood where they didn't really want us."

Packing their belongings, the family relocated from Boston to Buffalo. There, his father, Harold, took on a new church assignment while Mark's mother, Claudia, found work as a nurse.

Mark, the middle child of three siblings, laughingly portrays himself as a youngster who was "pretty much reserved. I was always into something, but I was quietly into it," he explains.

"So, you know, I wouldn't say that I was a problem child or anything." He smiles. "But I got into my share of trouble. I wasn't a troublemaker; it was the average neighborhood fights. I wasn't the kind of person who would go out and try to start something, but I would stand my ground if I had to."

Mark recalls that one thing he never lacked for as a youngster was religious instruction. "I grew up in a home where I read, I guess, what you would call the equivalent of Sunday School lessons pretty much every day.

"And with the exception of going to kindergarten in a public school, I was pretty much in church schools all my life. And, you know, we always had family worship. So I had a really good idea of what Christ was like early on. I knew the Bible stories and I read the Bible verses."

But it wasn't until he began memorizing long passages from the Bible between the ages of eight and ten years old that he remembers getting a deeper sense of what Christianity was all about.

"This is while we were living in Buffalo, and it really intensified my knowledge of Christianity," he recalls. "I became acutely aware of specific things like the Ten Commandments and the fact that He died for us. Before this it was more of an intellectual kind of thing."

Although religion was a way of life for him, he staged a brief rebellion against all the religious tasks he was required to do to help his Seventh Day Adventist father.

"I didn't mind all the religion until I was about ten or twelve years old," he relates. "That's when my father started doing evangelistic meetings, chant meetings. And I was required to go to those meetings every day.

"And that . . . you know, that was the time when all the kids were out playing, and I had to run the projector in the tent every night. It was summer and everybody else was out playing, and I wanted to play.

"That's when I started despising the fact that my father was a minister, and that I was forced to be involved. Having to do that, and listen to the sermons—I heard them so often—it all started to become mundane."

Mark begrudgingly continued to assist his father at the revivals, but remembers that he felt as if the spiritual spark was gone. The accomplished singer believes he might have rebelled even further had it not been for his discovery of Buffalo's Emanuel Temple, where his father had taken on pastoral duties.

"It was a church that was just alive with music," he recalls. "I loved that church and the gospel music that was going on there. That church really gave me back my interest in religion and my strong musical roots.

"I didn't even know what gospel music was prior to that," he declares, "except for the fact that my father listened to 'Oh Happy Day' and some of the Hawkins albums that followed it. And I learned those songs. That's when I first started playing the piano as well. But still, the realness of gospel music hadn't hit me yet."

Recalling his days in the Emanuel Temple, Mark remembers the profound effect the gospel music he heard sung there had upon him. "There was real power in it," he declares. "It really felt good. And it touched something in me. It made something spark and come alive. So that's where gospel music started to cultivate in me."

Inspired by the music, Mark started singing with small groups of friends and with the church's children's choir. At the same time, he began teaching himself how to play piano. "I enjoyed that and I picked it up pretty much by ear," he asserts.

His newfound interest in music was encouraged by his parents, particularly by his mother, who was the church organist. "They even tried to get me to take some lessons back then, and I took about two years of piano," Mark recollects.

"But then I just got disinterested, although I was still

playing. And before I left that church school, the teacher at the school helped me to formulate the school song. That was the first time I actually wrote a song."

Once more, the family relocated, this time to his current hometown of Nashville, Tennessee. In Nashville, Mark first attended Madison Academy, a Christian high school, but found that he did not enjoy it there. "Madison just didn't do anything for me," he recalls. "I just thought that I could get a better educational experience someplace else."

In 1980, the teenager transferred to the Oakwood College Academy in Huntsville, Alabama, a fateful move that was to mark the beginning of his incredibly successful musical career.

It was at Oakwood that Mark encountered an old friend from the Emanuel Temple, Claude McKnight. McKnight had formed an *a cappella* quartet at the college, which one afternoon was rehearsing for a performance in a bathroom.

Mark walked by, heard them, and added his voice to the foursome. "They were doing a standard arrangement of a gospel song and I thought, 'How dry,' " he laughingly recalls. "So I improvised a fifth part. They tripped; their mouths dropped open and they just took me in."

Although the group, which today includes Mark's younger brother, Joey, went through personnel shifts as various members graduated from college, Take 6 managed to keep on performing. It was after playing at a Nashville showcase that the sextet was signed by Warner/Reprise Nashville.

Success came quickly for the gospel-based *a cappella* sextet, which emphasizes jazz harmonies. The release of Take 6's self-titled debut in 1988 resulted in the group's first three Grammys and first four Dove awards.

In the years to come, Take 6, rooted solidly in Christian lyrics and inspirational sounds, would win another four Grammys and three Doves.

The crowd-pleasing sextet with its unearthly *a cappella* singing soon began to collaborate with some of today's greatest secular and gospel artists—including Quincy Jones. Take 6 also found itself performing on a variety of film sound tracks, including Spike Lee's *Do the Right Thing* and John Singleton's *Boyz N the Hood*.

Despite such success and the sale of millions of records since it first began performing more than twelve years ago, Mark emphasizes that the sextet has never compromised its gospel roots.

"Everytime we're invited to provide vocal backup, we always have to look through the lyrics to make sure that they are spiritually sound," the gospel star proclaims. "Our focus remains consistent: that we're part of a ministry."

Mark remains convinced that "God is running Take 6's career," a statement he is fond of repeating. The lead tenor further believes that the Almighty has always kept a personal eye on him as well.

He illustrates that point by sharing a story about a particularly stressful period in his life when the Lord assisted him. Mark relates that this occurred while he was attending college and learned that his parents planned to separate.

Feeling helpless to do anything about the situation, Mark recalls that he became filled with anger. He began to turn to alcohol to help ease the pain he was feeling.

"Things, you know, got kind of rocky at home," he relates. "My parents were going through some things and I was out there and trying to change that . . . and if I had stayed on that path it would probably have led me to some pretty crazy places.

"They were going through what a lot of parents go through—you know, the midlife crises where they discover what they thought was there between them actually wasn't. So they started having their troubles."

Mark was working toward his degree in Business Administration at the time, while performing with Take 6 and a second group. The teenager was living with his grandmother, a woman to whom he gives much credit for helping him to keep his life together during those unsettling months.

"Praise God for grandmothers," the talented vocalist declares, "because they pray for you no matter what's going on. You know, she was probably the one that kept me from really falling into some deep trouble.

"I was kind of thrust into trying to solve my parents' problems for them, which really led me to being half-crazy—'cause as a kid you can't solve those kinds of problems. And I was angry at what was happening to them."

As a result, the son of a minister recalls becoming "kind of wild. I started drinking, and coming home all hours of the night, and just trying different things. I never got into drugs. And I was too scared to smoke, because I had asthma. But I was hanging with the wrong crowd.

"I'd be out way too late at night—you know, getting into trouble with friends. And that was probably the part of my life where I was the furthest away from the Lord. I was a teenager and I was going through what a lot of teenagers go through. I was just kind of testing my wings, trying all kinds of things."

Although his behavior displeased his devoutly religious grandmother, the gospel star remembers how Thelma would nevertheless greet him each morning with a loving smile and without any recriminations.

"She'd make me breakfast, and whether I was listening or not, she would read a devotion. And a lot of times I wasn't listening at all, but she'd sit there and read it to me anyway.

"And she'd pray right there. And, you know, a lot of it just stuck. It was a constant reminder. Her famous words—and she still tells me them to this day—were, 'Just stay close to the Lord.' "

Adding to his personal problems, Mark's soul was divided over which career he should follow. Should he continue singing with Take 6 or enter the world of business? In the midst of all this stress, Mark believes he had an encounter with an angel.

"There was a guy in the Take 6 group—I can't even remember his name—and he realized that we had a lot of spiritual potential, even when we didn't. We were just kinda singing what was fun.

"It was like he had this power to see the future. He had us read this chapter in Matthew that talks about the Crucifixion. And he had us read it every day for a week. And he told us: 'Look, you know, you're gonna do some things that you probably will never believe you're gonna do. So just do this.'

"And we read it every day, over and over and over again. And, you know, I felt, 'Well, I don't even know what this is all about, him telling us to do this, but just let me do it. And I did it, and my life changed. My life changed, right then and there."

It was a remarkable turn of events. Today, Mark is convinced that this was, indeed, a clear case of divine intervention. "Yeah, I think He definitely sent him, 'cause, man, I don't know what would have happened to me had that particular experience not happened."

As Mark continued to read the recommended Scripture, he remembers how all his boiling anger over his parents' impending separation began to slowly evaporate.

"It really hit me internally," he declares. "I kept reading about the Crucifixion over and over: how Christ died, what He went through, what He said, what was going on around Him, how the weight of the world was on His shoulders—and all of that for me."

His spiritual life deepened beyond a reading of Scripture. "There were a lot of things at that college that could help you spiritually," Mark recalls. "Oakwood was just that kind of school.

"I mean every day they had 'Power Hour,' where you could just go and have a very strong worship service and be fed spiritually. And I started attending."

The "angel," however, was not quite through yet with Mark and other members of Take 6. "The next step he had us do was read John 3:16 over and over again, until something came and hit us inside.

"And you know, that's when things became real for me. And the problems that were going on at home . . . I realized then that I couldn't solve them, and that I had to just give them to the Lord, and let Him work them all out. I learned that you have to lean on the Lord for everything. He's the one that can solve them, He's the one that can pull everything together."

Mark abruptly began to curtail his bad behavior. The drinking stopped, as did his hanging out with friends all hours of the evening. Now there was only one person the teenager was interested in hanging out with: Jesus Christ!

"Once this happened, there was an experience that went along with it," he declares. "It was an experience that took me away from things that would separate me from the Lord, like drinking. Now I just didn't want to be separated."

The changes in him did not go unnoticed. "My grandmother sensed it; everybody around me sensed it," the accomplished singer recollects. "I was gone from her at the time. I was staying at the college. But she could tell something was going on. She could always tell," he adds with a laugh.

Even when his parents finally separated, Mark now viewed it as being for the best. "They continued to have their problems, until they finally did separate," he relates.

"But you know, praise God, things have been much better for them since then. God has brought very valuable people into their lives, and they've been able to move on and be very civil with each other."

Mark believes the "angel" who so mysteriously injected himself into his life was responsible for yet another improvement: Mark and his group were now all singing with more spiritual fervor than ever before. And their audiences were responding to it.

"Before, I would sing gospel just because it was the thing to do," he offers. "It was all right to sing gospel and I was in the environment where that's pretty much the only thing that was accepted, anyway. "But now we were singing what we were living."

Having quelled one demon of anger, another quickly arose to take its place. Again, the talented performer found himself locked in a struggle between choosing Christ-like gentleness or devil-induced anger. It was the devil who won, at first, Mark recalls.

"As life would have it, the devil put up more serious blocks in my life then," Mark recollects. "You know, there was a social thing going on around the college at the time where people were getting accused of homosexuality—it was like a witch trial. Homosexuality was coming out, and then AIDS came out, so, you know, it created the whole homophobic thing."

Mark, who hung out with a creative crowd, counted among some of his friends several classmates who were thought to be gay. As a result of that association, fingers began pointing at him as well.

"It would make me angry, you know, to be accused of something like that when I knew full well that homosexuality was not part of my life—not even close. I had always had girlfriends."

Reflecting back, what still saddens Mark the most about that time is that he turned his anger against those friends as well as his accusers.

"I felt that being around people who might look like they were into that kind of thing cast a shadow on me," he admits. "So I didn't want to have anything to do with anybody that looked like they might be that way.

"There was one guy that used to play the piano really, really well, and later in life he ended up dying of AIDS. When I was in college, that was one of my friends. And I no longer wanted to have anything to do with him."

There was one morning when Mark gazed into a mirror and was repulsed by the reflection staring back at him.

"I knew I had to get a real grip on things," he submits. "The way I was feeling was something that definitely shouldn't have been there. The Lord didn't want that in my life. The Lord didn't want me to be angry and hate people. I was hating everyone because of the accusations.

"But I just needed to be the tough guy that would never be accused of anything like that. I was angry enough to try to become like that kind of person. But by the same token, it was something that I didn't understand. And that's part of what made me angry all the time. So I had to find the Lord again."

Mark remembers talking things over with other members of Take 6, and how they made him aware that his anger was deeper than just his reaction to the events surrounding him.

"It wasn't just being angry with people, it was not knowing what life was gonna deal me in the future," he reflects. "I was studying business and singing with two groups.

"I felt unsure about what to do. The Lord was leading me someplace, but I didn't know what He was doing. It was confusing. Things got a little crazy there for a while."

What his fellow singers—all of them from religious backgrounds—advised their friend to do was turn to the Scriptures. They believed that Mark was under some kind of satanic attack.

"Well, what I learned from the group was that this was just something that the devil set up to confuse me and take me away from the Lord. You know, it was a hard thing for me to deal with, but I dealt with it nonetheless, even though it diverted my attention from the Lord.

"I got back into the Word. And it was at that point that a real big light hit me, and I started reading in First John about love—what love was all about. And that changed my life again. And it took away some of the hatred and the anger that I had.

"I realized that, first of all, God is love, and He requires you to love everybody, no matter what they're going through. Sin is sin. We're all full of sin. Yet God loves us. God requires that we love Him with all our heart and with all our soul and with all our mind, and that we love our neighbor as ourselves. And your neighbor is everybody."

The more he studied the Bible the more Mark felt relief from the intense anger that was threatening to overwhelm him. "I began to realize that everything you do for Christ should come from the motivation of love.

"So at that point I began to pray: 'Oh, Lord, just teach me how to love, because, you know, I got a lot of anger up in me.' And I saw my life change, again, in a miraculous way.

"A lot of the homophobic side of me left at that point. A lot of the anger that I had toward the finger pointers left me at that time. And even some of the anger I still had left for my parents also left me."

Today, Mark remains grateful at how the Lord intervened in his life on both those occasions. He adds with a smile that there was yet another time when he felt touched by God.

Mark relates that this happened shortly after his marriage to his current wife, Sherry, a former backup singer for BeBe and CeCe Winans.

"She wasn't a Seventh Day Adventist, and she brought a whole new light into my life," he declares. "I had grown up always falling to the Word for spiritual enlightenment and a spiritual jump-start.

"Sherry couldn't do that. She needed a church atmosphere to do this. So we'd go to the churches, and a lot of Adventist churches are very conservative, and we were trying to find the most nonconservative church we could find.

"And we finally found one that's filling our needs now. But we also attended a few other churches around the city that are not Adventist. And it was in one of them that I had a spiritual experience that changed my life for me."

Mark emphasizes that what he underwent in that church was something he had never felt before. "It was different from how I felt after reading the Word," he recalls. "The spirit fell and fell on me those times when I read the Word, but it didn't fall on me the same way.

"I walked into that church and it was so emotional, it came from the inside and went to the outside. I knew the spirit had hit me 'cause everything around me just seemed to vanish. I went into a phase where there was nothing but me and the Lord. I was swept away by it all—and I still am."

Mark advises that anyone gripped by anger can rid themselves of such violent feelings by seeking out the

Almighty. "Just ask the Lord into your life and He will come. Just be prepared to receive Him.

"It might be through a church; it might be through the Word; it might be through a person. I don't know how the Lord's gonna come into your life. But when you ask for Him, He'll be there. He's got His hand out there all the time, it's up to you to reach out and grab it. You've got to make the effort."

He also counsels not to be discouraged about seeking the Lord because of how impossible a certain situation may seem.

"No matter what the circumstances you find yourself in, it's just a matter of holding your hand out to Him," Mark declares. "He'll pull you through whatever the circumstance is because he loves you more than anything else in the world."

Reaching out for the Lord's hand is something Mark attempts to do daily through prayer. "I pray every morning, and I try to have worship with my wife every day as well. And I pretty much pray anytime, anywhere.

"Sometimes it's on my knees, sometimes it's sitting down, sometimes it might be in my car—you know, with my eyes wide open." He laughs. "I want the Lord to walk with me, and I want to be able to talk to Him anytime, anywhere. I want Him to be just like a friend that's always by my side. Being able to pray like that makes me acutely aware of His presence."

The welfare of others is also part of his prayers, the talented performer reveals. "That's something I've gotten into lately," he declares. "And if I tell someone I'm gonna pray for them, I'm gonna pray for them.

"You know, a lot of our prayers tend to be selfish, because we need so many different things. But when you pray for others, somehow the prayers are different. Reaching out to pray for someone else helps to change you."

As for the future? Well, that's an easy question for Mark to answer: "We want to continue to get the message out and make some beautiful music doing it," he replies.

"We want to continue singing the message that it's God we serve and God that we love so much, because He so much loves us. We want to keep singing about these sentiments of our hearts."

VICKIE WINANS

Photo by Marty Griffin

How do you write about someone who has become a jewel in your life? Vickie is just that, a jewel in my life. The closest I've observed Vickie was at the death of her father. When I received the call, I immediately flew to Detroit to be with the family.

As the family gathered, Vickie's role became evident. She was quite organized, attentive, caring, and supportive to each individual that she needed to communicate with. By the way, Vickie's brothers and sisters are also very talented. Some of them sing and play musical instruments. Tim Bowman, her brother, is an accomplished guitarist and recording artist.

I love the fact that Vickie is so touched with class and grandness. Style is reflected in her million-dollar mansion, her superb wardrobe, her videos, her CD projects. It all adds up to a soldier for the Lord having the best.

Vickie's sense of humor has garnered her a tremendous following. When I observe her in various music settings, she always comes to the table both with that humor and a strong sense of the needs of the people. Her belief in Christ is strongly exhibited in her tireless efforts to save souls, inspire, and heal sin-sick hearts.

Vickie's business acumen is also very keen. I am sure she would impress Wall Street easily. I am delighted to share Vickie Winan's testimony with you.

near-fatal illness and a painful divorce from her husband, singer Marvin Winans, twice brought four-time Grammy nominee Vickie Winans to her knees begging for God's help.

And on both occasions the Detroit native, who began her singing career at age six, gratefully recalls that her prayers were answered.

Today, the CGI Records star, who at one point doubted she would survive her illness, continues to sing the good news of Jesus Christ. The veteran performer, known for her warm spirit and natural humor, uses her soulful, finely tuned voice as an instrument to uplift the spirits of others who are in need, as she once was.

"It may feel like you don't have a lot, or you may feel like you're not gonna come out of it, the award-winning performer declares. "But if you just hang in there, and hold on, the Lord will deliver you."

Vickie, who has always clung to her faith, is at the moment celebrating her latest blessing: a Grammy nomination for her Stellar Award–winning album, *Live in Detroit*. Her enthusiasm cannot help but bring a smile to the face of anyone familiar with her life story.

The obstacles that this awesome talent has endured over the years—the latest being the death of her father just before she finished recording her Grammy-nominated album—at times made it doubtful that she would even be around today to celebrate her latest achievement.

At age twenty-nine, Vickie says, she became so critically ill that "I thought I wasn't gonna make it. It was a gallbladder disorder, but the doctors didn't know at the time what was wrong with me. I really thought I was gonna die. I went down to about a hundred pounds."

Besides being frightened, Vickie remembers also being embarrassed by her mystery illness. "I was just really disheartened. You know, they couldn't find out what it was, and I was losing all this weight.

"And, after a while, when you're sick long enough, you get embarrassed. You think you're not going to be healed and that everybody's thinking, you know, what did you do wrong, and this and that, because the Lord isn't healing you? It left me questioning why I wasn't being healed. I had always been faithful to God."

Although she was deathly ill and disappointed that the Lord had not sent her a healing, Vickie now, upon reflection, is proud of the fact that during that ordeal she never once blamed or criticized God for what was happening to her.

"I was never angry at Him even though I was sick for nine, almost ten months, and I really thought I was not going to live," she recalls. "My body weight went down to almost nothing. I couldn't eat anything."

It was her mother's words that helped to strengthen the young entertainer during this crisis. "I remember she once told me, 'Never lose faith in God because He works in His own time.'

"So I didn't grow angry at Him for not healing me. I knew that if He didn't heal me, it didn't mean that He wasn't able to heal me. He just had something else in mind for me. And I thought that if He took me home, it would be to a better place than this.

"If I died, it meant that He wanted me to come live with Him forever. So I couldn't lose. The Scripture says: To be absent in the body is to be present with the Lord.

"And that, right there, lets you know if you die, you're gonna be with Jesus; and there'll be no more pain, and no more suffering, and no more sickness and all that.

"I've been through this and through two divorces, and there's been nothing in my life to cause me to get angry at God or want to leave him. God has never done a thing to me except to uplift me, bless me, and nurture me through heartaches that come with life itself."

Her firm foothold on faith is a result of a strong spiritual upbringing. The seventh of twelve children, the versatile vocalist recollects that "we were a very close family. There was a wonderful spiritual environment at home, with lots of prayer, lots of spiritual talk, and we sang, sang, sang all the time. That was the order of the day."

Vickie, who today lives in Bloomfield Hills, Michigan, with her two sons, Marc "Skeeter" Winans and Marvin "Coconut" Winans, doesn't remember whether her childhood southwest Detroit neighborhood was dangerous or not.

"I just remember that it wasn't a poor neighborhood, and it wasn't upper class, and that we had nice people living on our block. And the school was just up the block, so we didn't have to go too far. I didn't even know what the northwest side of Detroit looked like until I was nineteen or twenty years old."

Blessed with a God-given gift for music, Vickie, who began singing at age six and sang her first church solo when she was only eight years old, believed as a child that all families shared her family's way of life.

"As a child, I thought that religion and music was how everyone lived because that was all I knew," she laughingly recalls. "I thought that everybody lived like we lived. So when us kids got older, it was kind of a surprise to learn that people didn't quite live the life that we lived.

"You know, they partied, and smoked, and drank and did a lot of things, like drugs and stuff. We had no idea that kind of stuff was going on. We were protected from it, you know?"

Chuckling at the memory, Vickie relates that through most of her formative years she believed that drugs and alcohol were only part of white society. "You know, we'd see people doing that on TV, but at the time it was only white people who were on TV.

"So I thought that's who was basically doing that kind of stuff. I thought at the time that the black race was just something special and different. I never saw black people on TV doing those kinds of things."

Today, Vickie remains grateful that she and her family were not exposed to alcohol and drugs. "I don't think I missed anything by not going to parties. I didn't really need to do that back then, and I still don't need to do that. My body's healthy because we didn't have drugs and alcohol going on in our lives."

Instead, it was music that preoccupied her most of the time, the gospel star recalls. Vickie remembers that even as a kid, she felt confident that her singing skills were something special.

"Even back then you couldn't tell me I wasn't ready for Carnegie Hall." She laughs. "I was just blessed with a voice." What the future gospel star did not realize back then is that, one day, she actually would perform at that world-famous concert hall.

Vickie remembers how she never tired of singing. Even when she was not performing in church, the youngster managed to find a way to be in the spotlight.

It wasn't packed Carnegie Hall audiences that she was playing to back then, but her next-door neighbors who would often gather outside her house to listen to Vickie and the rest of her musically talented family sing gospel songs.

"We'd have our windows open and people would be in the alley and on the side of the house just listening to us sing," she says, chuckling.

Vickie recalls deciding to pursue a career as a musician at age sixteen. "I sang in family groups and in church groups. And I loved Andrae Crouch. I loved the quality of the work that he did. So we mimicked his group.

"And I loved Tramaine Hawkins and the Hawkins Family. I just loved that group. And they gave me the inspiration and the drive to want to do what they were doing. And so it all started to come together."

Another person whom Vickie credits for encouraging her talents is Charles O. Miles, then pastor of the International Gospel Center, a Pentecostal church that Vickie and her family attended. "He was my pastor for twenty years and he always told me that I could sing professionally," she recalls.

It was through her church singing that Vickie met and fell in love with Marvin Winans, who was a member of the famous Winans singing group. For a while, she recalls concentrating more on her marriage than her musical career, supporting Marvin in his efforts as an artist.

After giving birth to her two sons, Vickie decided to get back to what she loved doing the most: performing. She became a member of the Winans Part II, a group that included her husband and two of today's greatest gospel stars: CeCe and BeBe Winans.

It was the success of that group that launched Vickie's career. With Marvin's help, Vickie then recorded a demo of her own, and a recording contract on the Light Records label followed.

Her first album, *Be Encouraged,* which included Vickie's signature song, "We Shall Behold Him," was a stunning success. The album went on to win the talented young artist her first Grammy Award nomination.

That record also earned her a Stellar Award for Album of the Year and an Excellence Award for Best Female Contemporary Artist.

Vickie's 1988 release, *Total Victory*, was another record that made it to the top of the gospel charts, and the gifted young entertainer from the streets of Detroit felt she was living a fairy-tale existence.

But Vickie's life was not a children's book, and a happy ending was not guaranteed the way it is in those kinds of stories. In 1995, at age twenty-nine, Vickie suddenly found herself in the midst of a painful divorce.

"That was something that was very challenging and very stressful to me and it threw my body way off course," she recollects. "I didn't know that mental stress could have such a physical result. But I hurt real bad, I went into a state of depression, and I started to gain weight."

Vickie won't discuss the specifics of her breakup, stating only that, "I have nothing negative to say about Marvin. That's my baby's daddy and the father of my son. And after a while in a relationship it doesn't matter who's at fault. When you break up you let the devil come in and trick you."

What she is willing to talk about is the "heartache, pain, and depression" that she succumbed to in the aftermath of her divorce, and how God touched her at that sorrowful time.

"I was invited to sing by Bishop T. D. Jakes at one of his revival meetings," Vickie relates. "He was holding a 'Woman, Thou Art Loosed' service in Lakeland, Florida. I think it was the summer of 1995."

Although still deeply depressed over her divorce, Vickie remembers being unable to refuse the popular evangelist and singer's request for her to perform the title song from his best-selling album, *Woman, Thou Art Loosed,* at his revival service.

"I wasn't feeling well, but people never stopped calling me to ask me to perform," she relates. "And regardless of how badly I was feeling, I sang then just as much as I do now. All the pain of what I was going through was still there, but I had to work, and people were calling me to ask me to perform."

When she stepped onstage the evening of her performance, what Vickie recalls seeing was a sea of admiring faces who had no idea of the pain and sadness she was feeling.

"So I sang my song and then I sat down in one of the seats while Bishop Jakes preached. He was one of the most prolific and wonderful preachers I'd ever heard in my entire life. And he was preaching, and he was talking about a bride. And I was crying."

In a movement that surprised her, the evangelist suddenly strode over to the weeping singer and began wiping away her tears with a towel. To this very day, the memory of what happened next still stirs the talented entertainer.

"The moment he touched me with the towel, my entire body went limp, and I fell forward. And while I was down there lying on the floor, the Lord just spiritually operated on me and got my life back together. When I got up from the floor I was a brand-new person."

Vickie pauses, still moved by that memory. "My whole mental state suddenly came back to normal," she joyfully proclaims. "Things that were wrong with my body returned to normal. I started to lose weight—my body size had doubled—and I became like a fireball. My depression was lifted. And to this day nobody can stop me."

Since then, the accomplished singer has shared her testimony with thousands of her fans. "That's why I say if you're sick, if you're feeling pain, or if you're depressed, to continue to trust in God. But, first of all, try not to let stress work you over.

"Don't let the devil stress you out. You know, it may feel like you don't have a lot, or you may feel like you're not gonna come out of something, but if you just hang in there, if you hold on and keep your faith, the Lord will deliver you out of any situation.

"Cast your cares upon the Lord because He cares for you. A lot of times we want to carry our own burdens, but this is what causes our bodies to go out of whack. But if you cast your cares upon the Lord, He will deliver you."

Vickie offers that she applies that message to her own life. One of her favorite prayers, she discloses, is "God lifts the burdens of anyone who is suffering."

The gospel star's prayer life is an intense one, she confirms. "When I pray, I first of all get on my knees thanking Him, because He's just been so good to me. Sometimes God is so good to me I feel like an only child, though I know He's got millions and zillions of them.

"And I'm so grateful for His mercy and His grace. And I'm grateful that He died for me. So when I'm on my knees, before I start asking Him for anything else, I start out by thanking Him. And then I ask Him to help His people everywhere. And then I praise Him and thank Him again.

"You know, to be perfectly honest with you, God works on so many situations in my life, that I don't have too much to ask anymore. He already knows, He just knows my situations. He's just such an on-time God."

Because of her busy schedule, the faith-driven vocal powerhouse attests that it is not always possible for her to pray at home—so she will pray anywhere! "I can be walking through the airport, in cars, planes, hotels—you name it—and I'll take some time out for prayer."

She also prays before taking the stage. "I give Him my all in every show that I do," Vickie emphasizes. "So that's another time of special prayer for me. And then I pray at night, too."

Looking ahead, Vickie says that she would like to increase her church ministry work, something her busy schedule makes it difficult for her to do right now.

"I wish I could be more than one Vickie Winans," she declares. "Then I could do more. Like right now I'm getting ready to go on this ninety-city tour, and it just takes up so much of my time.

"I'm doing quite a bit of ministry work, but I would like to do more and help more and more people. What I'd really like to do is fill baseball stadiums with people praising the Lord."

The gospel great is not shy about seizing any opportunity to spread the Word of God. It has even led the personable performer, known for her warm spirit and natural humor, to the theatrical stage on such a quest.

Over the years, Vickie has starred in several hit musicals, including the Broadway production of *Don't Get God Started*. Other productions she has appeared in are *The First Lady, Perilous Times,* and *The Christmas Celebration*. Each of these plays, she points out, is carefully selected to make certain that it offers a positive spiritual message.

In addition, for the past ten years, Vickie has hosted the nationally syndicated television variety show, *Singsation,* which she submits offers "positive and new talent to the public." The versatile artist also serves as the national spokesperson for the Quaker Oats Company's Voices of Tomorrow Youth Gospel Choir Competition.

Whether it's a Trinity Broadcasting Network performance, an appearance on a television gospel program, or by way of radio, albums, and videos, Vickie's ministry is a blessing to the hearts of millions everywhere.

"I absolutely love what I do," she exclaims. "God has given me a lot of opportunity to spread His word in different ways. I've been offered movie roles and gospel talk shows, and I'd like to do more television.

"I'm just having a ball doing the will of God! The Bible says that a 'merry heart doeth good like a medicine.' I'm trying to make it safe to laugh and worship in the same setting."